REFORMING FINANCIAL SYSTEMS

Recent Titles in
Contributions in Economics and Economic History

REFORMING FINANCIAL SYSTEMS

POLICY CHANGE AND PRIVATIZATION

Neal S. Zank,
John A. Mathieson,
Frank T. Nieder,
Kathleen D. Vickland,
and
Ronald J. Ivey

CONTRIBUTIONS IN ECONOMICS AND ECONOMIC HISTORY,
NUMBER 127

GREENWOOD PRESS
New York • Westport, Connecticut • London

Library of Congress Cataloging-in-Publication Data

Reforming financial systems : policy change and privatization / Neal S.
   Zank . . . [et al.].
      p. cm.—(Contributions in economics and economic history,
   ISSN 0084–9235 ; no. 127)
      Includes bibliographical references and index.
      ISBN 0–313–28100–9 (alk. paper)
      1. Banks and banking—Government ownership. 2. Financial
   institutions—Government ownership. 3. Privatization. I. Zank,
   Neal S. II. Series.
   HG1725.R44 1991
   332.1—dc20   91–20043

British Library Cataloguing in Publication Data is available.

Library of Congress Catalog Card Number: 91–20043
ISBN: 0–313–28100–9
ISSN: 0084–9235

First published in 1991

Greenwood Press, 88 Post Road West, Westport, CT 06881
An imprint of Greenwood Publishing Group, Inc.

Printed in the United States of America

The paper used in this book complies with the
Permanent Paper Standard issued by the National
Information Standards Organization (Z39.48–1984).

10 9 8 7 6 5 4 3 2 1

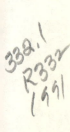

Contents

Tables and Figures

Preface

This book presents approaches and guidelines that can be utilized by government officials, private sector leaders, and aid donors to privatize government-owned financial institutions or liberalize developing country financial systems. We have sought to provide relevant, timely, and useful information in an effort to turn the decision-making framework away from one that is government-directed and toward one that is based upon the competitive, free marketplace. We also hope that those concerned about privatization, international economics, and financial systems development will find this book of interest and value.

This book is the result of a research project conceived in mid-1988 at the U.S. Agency for International Development. The Office of Policy Development and Program Review (PDPR) in AID's Bureau for Program and Policy Coordination was pursuing a research program titled "Privatization Policy Studies." PDPR sought to expand its privatization research in order to develop policy and other approaches that could help AID's overseas Missions pursue privatization programs in different development fields. The privatization of developing country financial systems and institutions was identified as a critical target for research.

To accomplish its study, PDPR relied upon a Private Enterprise Development Support contract between AID's Bureau for Private Enterprise and Ernst and Young. SRI International, a subcontractor under that contract, was selected to prepare the report. The final report was completed in December 1989, and entitled "Liberalization and Privatization of the Financial Sector: Guidelines and Case Studies." The authors of this book were involved in either the original conception or preparation of the report.

In early 1990, the authors determined that the subject of the report would be of interest to a broader population than AID personnel. Our attempt to expand and enhance the discussion resulted in a book that differs from the original report in three significant ways. It provides an expanded discussion of the purposes and characteristics of developing country financial systems. It also offers more evidence on the public/private debate and the greater efficiency associated with private sector financial institutions. Finally, we have attempted to remove or explain as much technical language as possible in hopes that readers without a technical background will understand both the primary issues and the possible solutions that we present.

The authors wish to thank Danette Kesner of SRI International for her assistance in report production and Robert Rourke of Ernst and Young for his support of the original project.

The findings and recommendations presented in this book are solely those of the authors and not those of the U.S. Agency for International Development, SRI International, or Ernst and Young. Of course, any errors presented in this volume are the responsibility of the authors.

REFORMING FINANCIAL SYSTEMS

1 Introduction: The Two-Pronged Strategy of Financial Reform and Privatization

The central objective of this book is to help government officials, private sector leaders, and donor agency professionals bring financial systems into a framework in which decisions and performance are driven by market forces rather than by government directive. The book provides analysis and practical guidelines for efforts to reform capital and credit markets and to privatize government-owned and operated financial institutions in developing countries. The findings and recommendations presented in this book build both on studies of actual bank privatizations and on current literature.

One of the primary constraints to accelerated economic performance in developing countries is the absence of strong, dynamic financial systems. Healthy capital and credit markets can serve the vital functions of attracting savings, intermediating funds, and allocating credit to productive uses. Development practitioners are unanimous in their identification of capital formation as one of the most important components in the development process.

Many if not most developing countries suffer from repressed financial systems that have been battered by the worldwide debt crisis and subjected to excessive regulation and government interference. Until these markets are released from such conditions and allowed to carry out their appropriate functions, entire economies will suffer.

Unfortunately, financial systems are often overlooked by development practitioners since their structures are viewed as arcane. Also, their problems are seen by donor agencies as too large to tackle. Relatively limited energies have been expended in designing and implementing systematic reforms oriented toward increasing domestic capital formation and financial intermediation. In addition, traditional development assistance has focused on either the "productive" sectors of agriculture and manufacturing or on sectors which provide essential services—health, education, sanitation, housing, and so forth. Relatively limited attention has been given to developing effective financial systems that ultimately serve all of these sectors. Financial systems should be considered important economic sectors in themselves. Finance is a means to an end.

This development oversight is particularly disturbing because debt-ridden developing countries enjoy almost no access to international capital markets. They have witnessed declines in official financial flows and have attracted only limited amounts of private direct investment. If these nations are to have any chance of achieving pre-oil and pre-debt crisis growth rates, they must generate higher levels of domestic capital formation, reduce leakages from the system through capital flight, and entice the repatriation of funds already transferred offshore. To meet these requirements, domestic capital and credit markets must evolve in such a way as to provide necessary incentives and an appropriate policy environment for capital formation and retention.

This book suggests that laying a foundation of sound macroeconomic, sectoral, and regulatory policies conducive to financial sector development is, in most cases, the most important step to effective capital markets development. It should precede or at least accompany any privatization efforts. A concerted program of macroeconomic and regulatory reforms and privatization will encourage healthy financial sector development. Macroeconomic reforms (implementing positive real interest rates, controlling the government deficit, maintaining low inflation, and encouraging a competitive exchange rate) will create a context conducive to financial sector growth by encouraging saving and productive investment. Regulatory reforms, which include reducing directed credit and excessive reserve requirements, lifting interest rate ceilings, and improving bank supervision, will also bring about benefits such as a more efficient allocation of capital, greater domestic resource mobilization, and reductions in banking fraud.

As with financial systems, financial institutions themselves are often neglected by the "development community," in part because they act as intermediaries between two groups that are typically the recipients of development assistance programs and projects—the general public and the "productive" sectors of the economy. Development agencies tend to focus either on the poverty and needs of the general public or on the requirements of agriculture, industry, and other productive sectors. Much less attention is focused on the financial institutions serving as intermediaries between the two groups. In fact, all sectors benefit from healthy capital and credit markets, and similarly all sectors suffer from unstable or underdeveloped financial markets.

Government and privately-owned financial institutions can be expected to diverge on a number of areas of behavior and performance. Because of the incentive structure private banks face, they tend to be more efficient, offering higher quality service with lower administrative costs. Private banks also tend to respond more rapidly to opportunities to increase market share by introducing new, attractive financial instruments. They are generally more diligent about collecting loan payments. Mindful that in competitive markets, "the customer is king," private banks carefully cultivate confidential relationships with their clients, especially large depositors and borrowers.

On the other hand, managements of government banks are driven by other incentives and directives, many of which are politically rather than commercially motivated. As a result, loans are directed toward uneconomic but politically desired projects, and decision-making is bureaucratic. Staff sizes tend to be bloated and filled with unqualified and unmotivated personnel. Consequently, the performance of such banks and the economy as a whole suffer from inefficiency and inappropriate allocations of scarce capital.

The macroeconomic implications of bank ownership heighten the importance of bank privatization. Each of the divergences between publicly and privately owned institutions affects the efficiency and dynamism of the entire sector, and in turn, the economy as a whole. By providing incentives for efficiency and profitability, privatization will bring about many of the same benefits as reform, but also will encourage administrative efficiency and careful personnel recruitment and supervision, two benefits not created by reform. Each of these components— privatization, macroeconomic reform, and regulatory reform—can contribute to both improved financial sector performance and the achievement of national economic and social objectives.

Privatization does not refer to a single transfer mechanism, but to a host of alternative measures. One commonly cited reason for not privatizing is a lack of functioning capital markets. As the case studies in Appendix A indicate, many privatization options exist that do not require capital markets. They include corporatization, reduction of barriers to new private banks, and joint ventures with foreign banks.

Confidence in a product or service of an industry or non-financial service organization will certainly affect its sales and profits. In the case of a bank privatization, *lack* of confidence can erode the bank's deposit base and seriously impair the success of the privatization transaction. To be successful, privatization of a financial institution must offer equal or greater security to existing depositors. By comparison to a typical industry or service business, therefore, the privatization of a banking institution could have a far greater impact upon the economy as a whole.

Such factors lead one to conclude that bank privatization is a more delicate task than the privatization of other government-owned enterprises. There are four reasons for this conclusion.

- Anything that affects the financial sector reverberates and is often magnified in the rest of the economy because of the primacy of financial institutions in an economy.

- Many financial institutions accept deposits and, therefore, have a fiduciary responsibility to protect the deposits of savers. Savers have a clear and direct interest in the financial soundness and ownership of the institution over which they have little or no control.

- Any measures taken by government or private sector leaders that have the potential to undermine confidence in the system must be carefully planned and executed since confidence is a key factor in financial markets.

- Bank privatization, in comparison to privatization of nonfinancial entities, deals directly with money and the rapidity with which financial assets can be moved from one institution to another or even out of the country. Millions of dollars in local or hard currency can flow out of a financial system in a matter of days or hours in response to a government measure that appears threatening.

Privatization, in the absence of policy and regulatory reform, is no panacea for the myriad problems facing financial sectors in developing countries. A system characterized by negative real interest rates, an overvalued currency, extensive government credit controls, and ineffective bank supervision is likely to produce few discernible benefits. Nevertheless, privatization is an important tool available to developing country decision-makers for complementing financial liberalization and improving the performance and efficiency of the financial sector.

This report proposes a two-pronged approach to assist governments in avoiding these problems while designing reforms or privatization packages. The steps in the approach are as follows.

1. *Financial Sector Diagnosis.* The first task is to assess the current performance of both the formal and informal financial sectors, and determine the causes of system limitations.

2. *Policy and Institutional Targeting.* Once policymakers set overall goals, they should select key policy constraints to remove; and they should identify prime candidates for privatization, based on both technical and political criteria.

3. *Macroeconomic Reforms.* Policymakers should strive to create a policy framework conducive to financial sector growth. The desired environment should have the characteristics of positive real interest rates, low inflation, and a competitive exchange rate.

4. *Bank Regulation and Supervision Reform.* When necessary, the government should work toward lowering barriers to entry by private and/or foreign banks, reducing the scope of government-mandated portfolio allocation guidelines, and encouraging the use of standardized financial audits of banks and their clients.

5. *Privatization.* The lack of developed capital markets does not preclude privatization, given the host of alternative methods that exist. Any opposition to privatization should be closely monitored. Educational and promotional campaigns regarding the benefits of privatization should be launched. While widespread stock ownership is likely to engender popular support for privatization, it should often be tempered by assurances that institutional investors (such as pension funds, insurance companies, or foreign banks) hold a small but significant portion of total shares. The relatively large stake of institutional investors, combined with their technical knowledge of operating a financial institution, will improve oversight of management decisions.

Chapter 2 of this book provides a description of the operating components of financial markets in developing countries and an assessment of variables that collectively lead to underdeveloped or repressed financial markets. Chapter 3 presents evidence supporting the greater efficiency demonstrated by the private sector in performing banking functions. Chapters 4 and 5 describe the many facets of financial reform and privatization strategies.

These individual approaches are then pulled together in Chapter 6, where we discuss the criteria to apply in determining appropriate financial reform and privatization activities. Also presented are recommendations and a privatization checklist for use by development practitioners who wish to address the important issue of financial market development.

An appendix contains six country case studies of actual privatizations and accompanying policy reforms in the financial sector. These case studies seek to bring out the methods and strategies used to address financial sector reform in Bangladesh, Chile, Guinea, Jamaica, Mexico, and the Philippines.

2   An Overview of Developing Country Financial Systems

Financial systems play a critically important, central role in the activities of all economies. These systems carry out the important functions of clearing the exchange of goods and services as well as administering the aggregation and allocation of financial resources. Without some form of capital and credit markets, societies are limited to little more than barter economies. Financial sectors form the "circulatory systems" of and among agricultural, manufacturing, and other service sectors.

Within the financial system, specific institutions represent the organizational nucleus of capital and money markets and provide several essential services. Banks and other financial firms (savings and loan associations, brokerage houses, insurance companies, leasing firms, etc.) provide the public with a means to save for the future and to borrow to meet current financial needs. These organizations are the only way in which thousands of small investments from one set of "clients" can be transformed into short and long-term loans to fund the productive ventures of another set of "clients." Given the critical function that financial markets play in economic growth, financial reform and privatization of financial institutions merit careful consideration.

Financial systems appear complex for several reasons. First, the number of actors involved is large, and each holds different goals and responsibilities. Second, the range of instruments involved in financial transactions is often sufficiently broad to confuse even experienced participants. Third and most importantly, many economic, political, and even social variables come into play as both causes and effects underlying the dynamics of financial systems. This factor adds increasing layers of complexity to financial analysis and policy formation (see Figure 2.1).

Figure 2.1
Capital Markets Interactions

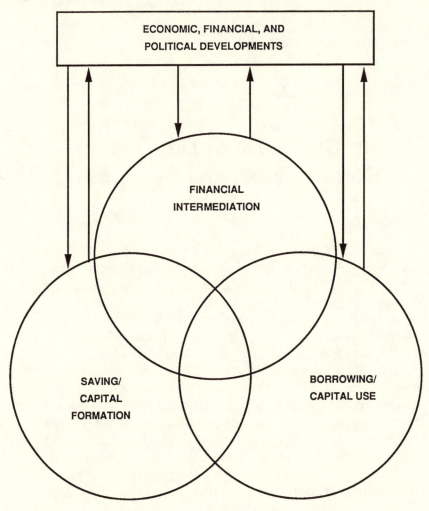

The most appropriate approach for addressing financial market issues is to begin with a description of the history of financial systems development, followed by a discussion of the functions of and actors in any financial system. This chapter then presents the basic operating components and forces at work in financial systems. It later incorporates additional factors (e.g., institutional, economic, policy, etc.) that come into play in the determination of financial conditions and processes. The chapter concludes with an analysis of the nature and impact of factors that retard growth in money and capital markets and give rise to a condition known as "financial repression."

FINANCIAL SYSTEM DEVELOPMENT

The evolution of financial systems in most countries has followed a common pattern, with strong interrelationships between the existing types of financial institutions and the forms of payment or mode of exchange. In almost all instances, however, a considerable time lag exists between modernization of the "real" economy (e.g., manufacturing, agricultural production, etc.) and development of the financial system.

In most countries, as incomes rise, financial systems grow to provide the wider range of services associated with the mobilization and allocation of resources. To provide these services, financial systems must offer to economic entities financial assets whose characteristics are sufficiently attractive that they can compete with holdings of physical capital as stores of wealth. The evolution of the means of exchange has followed a common pattern, moving from self-sufficiency, to barter, to trade for commodity money, to fiat money, to bank checks, and then on to more sophisticated forms of payment. As technology advances, credit and other sophisticated means of payment replace money to an extent.

Countries at an early stage of development typically have a small number of formal financial institutions, which are able to accumulate only a relatively small volume of local savings and that offer limited services. Therefore, the need for credit is served by a combination of formal institutions and the activity of informal private money lenders. Initially, the burden of financial intermediation falls mainly on private money lenders, particularly in the rural areas of developing economies. Many small and micro-enterprises borrow funds in the informal sector or from unofficial sources of credit that operate outside of normal financial institutions. This credit is short-term in terms of maturity but carries very high (and close to real) interest rates.

On the other hand, commercial banks generally provide only short-term, highly collateralized credit to serve the temporary needs of traders, artisans, and commercial farmers, allowing the commercial banks a high degree of liquidity and low risk. Commercial institutions also respond to the need of savers in the monetized portion of the economy who want high security and liquidity (usually in the form of checking accounts and, to a lesser extent, time deposits).

As economies grow and diversify, credit demand expands and becomes more complex. The expanding demand for physical capital (land, buildings, machinery, and infrastructure) results in commensurate increases in demand for credit that varies by the length of time required (short-, medium- or long-term) as well as the end use (consumer, investment, risk capital, venture capital, mortgage, etc.). Investments in industry, mining, transportation, and utilities typically require larger outlays of capital than the traditional lenders are accustomed to with their trading and agricultural clients.

The pace at which financial institutions evolve to satisfy the needs of a developing economy depends on a number of factors, including economic and political stability, the character of the local production, delivery and marketing systems, and supportive government policies. The capacity of financial institutions to carry out their responsibilities efficiently and profitably is a function of many considerations, including overall economic conditions, government policies and regulations, and forms of ownership and management control. The opposite causal relationship also holds. Financial sector performance can materially affect economic, social, and government policy developments. The most common forms of financial institutions are specialized institutions, such as agriculture or housing finance facilities, venture capital firms, and stock and bond markets.

When the pace of financial evolution occurs too slowly to satisfy the perceived demand for specialized or medium to long-term credit, developing country governments (often supported by donors) have attempted to fill gaps in their financial structure by sponsoring new financial institutions and specialized credit programs, often in the public sector. These developing countries seek to increase the depth of their financial system or to bypass the relatively slower or stalled institutional development process of the existing financial sector by channeling additional credit resources to specific target groups. They attract savings by providing individuals and firms with convenient collection points and appropriate, safe instruments at attractive rates. These or other institutions then transform the excess funds into instruments that meet borrowers' needs. Lastly, they lend the funds to individuals, firms, and projects deemed to have the ability to repay the loans and interest incurred. In addition to these banking functions, secondary markets provide financial instruments (equity, marketable securities, etc.) that can be distributed to a broad array of investors. Each of these functions is critical to efforts to assure an adequate supply and appropriate allocation of capital.

Typically, the commercial banking institutions in lower income developing countries are reluctant to enter into long-term loan financing for reasons that include their shallow resource bases, their preference for fast recovery of funds, their timidity about entering untried fields, their inexperience with term credit instruments, and limited local markets for large, long-term financial assets. Other factors that further inhibit their willingness to venture into new types of lending include failure to appreciate the potential profitability of the new opportunities, lack of familiarity with the new entrepreneurs, and scarcity of managerial and entrepreneurial talent needed to seek out, appraise, and supervise long-term investment credits. The commercial banks are generally reluctant to extend credit to small scale, low income producers for reasons that include their untested debt servicing capabilities and the high costs of handling a large volume of small loans. Often lagging in the development process are reliable accounting standards and practices; legal codes and regulations concerning the security of assets, title, transfer of property, taking possession of collateral on loans in default, and sharing ownership of assets; financial information systems; and related prerequisites for the vigorous growth of the financial sector.

THE BASIC ROLES OF FINANCIAL SYSTEMS

The primary role of the financial system is to mobilize resources for productive investment. It provides the principal means for transferring savings from individuals and companies to private enterprises, farmers, individuals, and others in need of capital for productive investment. Any domestic financial system is composed of three sets of activities: saving (capital formation), borrowing (capital use), and financial intermediation. Virtually all facets of financial activities relate to one of these three functions. Saving and borrowing are the fundamental functions of any financial system; intermediation joins one function to the other.

Participants in the system can engage in any combination of these functions. For example, at any given time savers are also likely to be borrowers. Individuals maintain both savings accounts and mortgages. Corporations place liquid assets in bank accounts and at the same time assume debt to finance new projects. National governments always carry both asset and liability positions. Similarly, financial institutions are involved in both saving and borrowing as well as in intermediation (see Figure 2.2).

Figure 2.2
The Structure of Financial Markets

Principal Sources of Capital	Financial Intermediation	Principal Uses of Capital
INSTITUTIONS	**INSTITUTIONS**	**INSTITUTIONS**
Households Corporations Businesses Foundations	Commercial Banks Development Banks Savings and Loans Credit Unions Insurance Companies Stock and Bond Markets Mutual Funds	Businesses Governments Households
INSTRUMENTS		**INSTRUMENTS**
Savings Accounts Certificates of Deposit Checking Accounts Equity Shares Government Bonds Private Bonds		Corporate Loans Consumer Loans Mortgages Equity Shares Government Bonds Private Bonds

Mobilizing Domestic Resources: Saving

Saving results from an excess of current income over current expenditures. A portion of current income is not consumed but rather is saved to support future consumption. Savings in turn are transformed into financial or nonfinancial assets that are often used, directly or indirectly, to create additional economic activities.

Well-functioning and well-developed financial systems encourage savings and allocate resources to higher-yielding investments. Savers can make their surpluses available to investors by, in effect, purchasing financial assets. The financial system mobilizes savings and increases liquidity by providing asset holders with attractive (in terms of yield, risk, and liquidity) financial claims. In the absence of developed financial systems, only investments financed by individual savers or closely-knit groups of individuals would be possible. Many high-yielding investments would not be undertaken, and some capital would be invested in activities yielding low returns.

All economic entities tend to experience periods of both saving and dissaving. In the case of individuals, debt is accumulated early in life to finance education and housing. This phase is followed by a period of net saving, during which previous debts are amortized and savings are accumulated for retirement, another period of dissaving.

Business entities encounter similar periods of dissaving and saving. It normally takes time for corporations to accumulate capital surpluses. As a result, start-up phases have to be financed by equity or debt since new business ventures or projects nearly always incur initial negative cash flows before net project receipts turn positive.

The typical cycle for sovereign nations tends to be the reverse. In early stages of development, nations often generate surpluses in trade because earnings from commodity exports exceed effective demand for imports. These trends are usually reversed as the growth process evolves, with countries borrowing funds and attracting investment inflows, partly to pay for needed imports not covered by export earnings and partly to finance development. Economies are often transformed into "mature creditor nations" as they advance relative to others in terms of capital and technology endowments. Capital inflows are replaced by outflows in the form of credit to and investments in comparably less developed countries.

World Bank data indicate that average savings rates vary considerably across countries. In 1986, for example, national savings performances (gross domestic savings as a percentage of gross domestic product

(GDP)) ranged between a low of 78 percent negative saving (dissaving) for Lesotho to a high of 40 percent saving for Singapore and Yugoslavia. National savings rates in 1986 averaged 21 percent for industrial market economies, 26 percent for upper middle-income developing countries, 17 percent for lower middle-income developing countries, and 7 percent for low-income developing countries (excluding China and India). China and India recorded a combined average savings rate of 30 percent.

Employing Capital Productively: Borrowing

For decades, development theorists closely associated economic growth with increases in nations' "capital stock," which in turn is dependent on capital formation. In practical terms, this term refers to the deployment of financial assets in productive activities—plants, machinery, infrastructure and physical assets associated with human welfare (e.g., housing, hospitals, schools, and so forth). Unless this "physical capital" is to be financed only from internally generated surpluses, which is seldom feasible, it must be developed on the basis of borrowed funds. The borrowing function is therefore central to the economic development process.

Borrowers seek funds for essentially three purposes: to purchase "consumption" items whose costs will be amortized over the productive lives of the borrowers; to finance temporary shortfalls in liquidity; or to finance the purchase of productive capital goods. To obtain funds for the initial two purposes, the borrower must convince the lender that he or she has sufficient general means to service debt repayments. In the case of funds sought to finance a project, the borrower must show that the proposed investment is viable. Over time, borrowers establish reputations regarding their willingness and ability to service financial obligations, and hence are assigned implicit or explicit credit ratings by lenders.

The key requirement of financial systems related to borrowing is to provide users of capital with access to funds at reasonable terms and conditions. In addition, systems should include rules and procedures to determine the creditworthiness of alternative borrowers and to offer lenders appropriate calculations of risk/reward tradeoffs. If conditions placed on borrowers are excessively onerous, the capital formation process will be retarded or adversely biased. Alternatively, if borrowing conditions are unreasonably lax, then undue risks are borne by lenders.

Facilitating Saving and Borrowing: Financial Intermediation

Financial intermediation represents the crucial "transmission belt" between saving and borrowing. Intermediaries aggregate savers and borrowers and transform financial assets into productive financial liabilities.

Financial institutions provide a wide range of services associated with the two functional roles of financial transactions: means of payment for the exchange of real resources and extensions of credit. With regard to the former, intermediaries operate money markets to carry out domestic or foreign exchange transactions, to guarantee payments via letters of credit or their equivalent, and to carry out the physical transfer of funds.

Turning to the allocation of credit, the role of institutions is to "intermediate" between, or match, the asset preferences of savers with the liability preferences of borrowers. Savers generally seek investments that offer high returns, are relatively liquid, have limited maturity, and do not carry high levels of risk. Borrowers, on the other hand, prefer lower interest rates and often desire longer maturities. The function of intermediaries, therefore, is to reach sufficient tradeoffs among these preferences to accommodate the objectives both of lenders and of borrowers. In addition, financial intermediaries provide markets of sufficient size and depth to permit participants to "shop" for alternative instruments and to maintain diversified instruments of assets and liabilities to spread risks. Most financial transactions entail some form of intermediation for purposes of both convenience and risk reduction.

Another way to mobilize domestic resources through intermediation is through the development of equity and securities markets. Equity financing provides an alternative to debt financing. It also offers new opportunities for investors and for broadening the ownership of economic assets.

The principal processes encompassed in intermediation are the following:

- *Capitalization* is the accumulation of sufficient capital through equity and retained earnings; it is important to maintain prudent loan/asset ratios.
- *Deposit taking* is required to assure a steady supply of fresh funds to cover cash outflows in the form of withdrawals and new loans, as well as to accommodate nonperforming loans.
- *Asset/liability management* is the essence of financial intermediation; it seeks to balance financial exposure in terms of liquidity, interest rates, currencies, and maturities in such a way as to maximize returns and minimize risks.

- *Maturity transformation* is the process of accommodating differences between the maturity preferences of depositors and borrowers in any market segment.

- *Underwriting* constitutes the function of orchestrating and sometimes guaranteeing the issuance of corporate equities, notes, and bonds and of placing these securities in primary and secondary markets.

- *Credit allocation* is the act of distributing available funds among a diversified group of borrowers in such a way as to maximize interest income under established standards for overall portfolio risk.

- *Loan portfolio management* is the administration of outstanding loans to assure prompt payment of principal and interest.

- *Fiduciary responsibilities* are those associated with the legal and ethical handling of funds on the account of clients.

Combining the savings and lending activities of financial intermediaries offers many benefits and demonstrates the importance of savings to institutional viability. It reduces some costs, including those of establishing creditworthiness, since financial intermediaries will have better information on and be better acquainted with borrowers through their role as savers. Saver-dominated financial institutions also tend to show steady growth in assets and liabilities, lower loan delinquency, and greater efficiency and financial viability. Borrower-dominated financial institutions tend to show higher rates of loan delinquency, poor rates of growth, perennial liquidity problems, and other weaknesses associated with dependence on external sources of funds.

Other Characteristics of Financial Systems

In addition to the three central functions noted above, financial systems carry out several important roles that affect not only capacity and strength of capital and credit markets themselves but also the economy as a whole. These roles include market efficiency and depth, and financial and economic integration.

Financial systems can be effective to the extent that they are efficient and deep. Efficient financial systems mobilize funds from savings with, at the margin, the lowest opportunity cost (adjusted for perceptions of risk). They then distribute those funds to investments that offer, at the margin, the highest potential returns (adjusted for perceptions of risk). Efficient financial systems also mobilize and allocate these funds at minimal cost. It is important to keep in mind that if there are inefficiencies in the market, then prices or costs would not reflect the real information relevant for financial decision-making.

The depth of financial systems is a measure of their strength; deep financial markets are inherently less fragile than shallow ones. In many developing countries, formal financial markets are shallow. Relatively few people have access to these markets, and the range of available financial instruments is limited. Friends, relatives, and moneylenders are the primary sources of external finance in such a system. Savings tend to be placed in real assets such as gold or cattle as a store of value. As the system develops, more options are available for yields, maturities, and risks, which leads to higher household welfare.

As the financial system develops, prospective investors increasingly can turn to local financial institutions, national financial organizations, and ultimately, international banks and securities markets for additional funds. Each step leads to a more efficient allocation of capital. The resulting increase in the availability of equity and debt funding will enable developing economies to move toward more balanced capital structures of enterprises.

Shallow, formal financial markets do not adjust well to external shocks without collapsing or displaying excessive fluctuations; they are markets in which severe gyrations are fairly common, institutions too often collapse, and "secure" instruments are not, in fact, safe havens for savings. Shallow financial markets also are rather easily subject to manipulation. Low-income developing countries, with their shallow financial markets, rely more heavily on administrative allocation systems than do high-income developing countries.

Financial systems also encourage financial and economic integration. Effective financial systems are integrated in two dimensions. First, integration can be "vertical." Vertically integrated financial systems are those in which the three principal market clusters (formal domestic markets, informal markets, and international markets) are closely linked. Second, integration can be "horizontal." Horizontally integrated financial markets are those in which market interest rates typically array themselves around a basic reference rate.

Vertically integrated financial systems incorporate informal and international financial markets with formal domestic financial markets. Informal financial markets are especially important in less developed countries (LDCs) because these markets provide the credit and savings mobilization functions for a major portion of the LDC population.

An effective financial market system should also connect domestic markets to international markets (and to the related commodity trading systems). The presence of effective financial markets in developing countries will encourage foreign investors to consider providing capital (in the form of both debt and equity) for productive investment. Over time, integration with international financial markets will narrow the differences in the cost of funds between markets in different countries and between different instruments, and spread the risks associated with exchange rate and interest fluctuations among a larger number of market participants.

In addition to stimulating financial integration, capital and credit markets also facilitate economic integration within and between countries. Banking and exchange operations support trade and investment transactions that could not proceed without financial intermediation. Integration allows for productive linkages among sectors, such as the aggregation of surpluses from "mature" sectors and allocation of capital to "emerging" sectors.

PARTICIPANTS IN FINANCIAL SYSTEMS

Although numerous actors are involved in the saving/capital formation process, the ultimate source of nearly all funds in financial markets is individuals. Individuals hold the claims to most financial assets, either directly from their own deposits, or indirectly through their explicit or implicit ownership of financial and nonfinancial institutions. Business corporations are for practical and sometimes legal reasons considered to be "individuals" regarding their rights and responsibilities, but even these entities are ultimately owned and controlled by individual stockholders.

For analytical purposes, one effective approach is to divide borrowers from and savers in financial markets into three classifications, households, businesses, and governments, capturing respectively the roles of individuals, business firms, and sovereign nations. Each of these "sectors" participates directly in capital and money markets, and in most countries each plays by a somewhat separate set of rules, based on common practices, capabilities, or legal and regulatory environments (see Figure 2.3).

The household sector consists of individuals and families, which for purposes of this analysis earn personal income, spend money to meet current consumption needs, save funds for future consumption, and borrow to acquire goods and services (e.g., housing, education, etc.) that cannot be financed from current income or accumulated savings. The business sector includes the entire array of private enterprises, each of

Figure 2.3
The Wide-Ranging Impact of Financial Markets

**Financial markets affect nearly all individuals
and all sectors in an economy:**

For households, financial markets:

✔ Facilitate transactions (checking accounts)
✔ Offer savings instruments
✔ Provide financing for consumption, homes, and education

For businesses, financial markets:

✔ Provide interest-paying instruments for excess cash
✔ Supply short-term credit to finance exports
✔ Dispense long-term credit for plant and equipment
✔ Provide start-up funds
✔ Place equity, notes, and bonds

For government, financial markets:

✔ Place government bonds with buyers
✔ Channel credit to high priority sectors

which not only generates income streams for owners and shareholders but also requires short-term credit to finance current transactions and long-term capital to invest in plant and equipment.

The government sector is composed of different levels of government (local, state or provincial, and national), which collect taxes and other revenues and provide public services such as public safety, education, infrastructure, health, national defense, and so forth. The provision of these and related services requires funds to cover both recurrent costs and capital expenditures.

The participants in the financial intermediation segment of money and capital markets include a wide range of official and private institutions, each of which plays a role in the processes of capital formation and allocation. The specific mix of institutional actors varies considerably by country, but it typically consists of the following types of institutions.

- *Government participants* include central banks, finance ministries, regulatory and supervisory agencies, and sometimes pension funds and other government-operated institutions.

- *Commercial banks* represent the core of most financial systems, and carry out the important functions of deposit taking, lending, and financial exchange transactions.

- *Investment or merchant banks* typically specialize in financial services for relatively large businesses, especially the orchestration of direct or syndicated lending and placement of equity, notes, and bonds.

- *Savings and loan associations* transform longer-term deposits into housing or personal loans for households.

- *Stock exchanges and brokerage houses* operate equity and money markets, providing secondary markets for the broad distribution of investment instruments.

- *Mutual fund companies* aggregate financial assets and liabilities and provide secondary market access to small investors.

- *Insurance companies* provide a range of insurance services and inject considerable funds into capital and money markets.

- *Institutional investors* include insurance companies and other groups (universities, pension funds, investment companies, trust funds, etc.) that manage collective portfolios seeking higher returns and asset growth than could be achieved by individual investors.

- *Venture capital companies* specialize in providing start-up funds to new ventures, either on a loan or equity basis.

- *Leasing companies* finance capital equipment (aircraft, vehicles, construction equipment, etc.) needed by private firms.

- *Factoring firms* purchase receivables at a discount or manage receivable collections.

In some financial systems, these different participants carry out specialized functions and are prohibited from engaging in others. The recent wave of financial market deregulation in many countries around the world has blurred these boundaries. Firms are increasingly eligible to expand the range of services they provide.

Governments play a key role in assuring that financial markets operate effectively. Governments in developing countries can facilitate financial markets development by providing an environment that encourages the emergence of competitive forces and a regulatory system that builds investor confidence while not impeding market development. They also should provide for the fair enforcement of contracts to protect investors, lenders, and borrowers, and support measures that encourage a variety of debt and equity instruments. Finally, governments should promote the growth of different institutions that offer a wide range of financial instruments and services to potential savers and investors. These institutions should protect the interests of savers by reducing their risks. Such actions would serve to decrease the transaction costs associated with financial intermediation.

FINANCIAL INSTRUMENTS

In many countries, savers have at their disposal a dizzying array of short-term and long-term financial instruments in which to place their surplus funds. Each carries a different mixture of risks, returns, and conditions. For example, individuals can hold cash, which maximizes liquidity but earns no interest and bears the risk of depreciation through price inflation or currency depreciation. Alternatively, they can hold a variety of instruments that earn greater returns but carry higher risks. These instruments enable individuals to make reasonable judgments about the risk and rewards of saving or investing their funds. They effectively package risk and returns so that individuals who wish to participate in appropriate markets can do so, taking into account their own perceived capacity to accept risk. Individuals are able to borrow funds on terms commensurate with the expected risk and return of the investments they wish to make.

A standard set of instruments for savers includes the following items. Call accounts or demand deposits may or may not earn interest. Time deposits are funds placed with banks for specified periods of time; callable savings deposits represent a hybrid of demand and time deposits. Bankers Acceptances are negotiable time drafts drawn to finance corporate operations, primarily trade or working capital funding. Certificates of Deposit are short-term or medium-term investment instruments issued by banks. Money market funds consist of a potpourri of alternative instruments that offer investors shares in portfolios of direct placements of funds. Equities represent shares in the ownership of corporations; they may or may not carry voting rights. Corporate notes and bonds are issued by private companies seeking to finance their operations. Debentures are a form of corporate bond that may be converted into equity. Finally, government securities constitute financial obligations of national, state, or local governments (or their equivalents), and include bills, notes, and bonds.

On the borrowing side of the equation, individuals tend to rely on mortgages, personal loans, and consumer credit to bridge their financing gaps. Corporations issue equities, notes, and bonds to raise capital in secondary markets, and they acquire direct loans from financial institutions and from other nonfinancial firms through intercompany loan markets. Governments issue the range of securities described above and in some cases borrow from international financial markets to cover budget deficits and capital expenditures.

Financial intermediaries utilize and manage all of the instruments described above, except direct placements of funds between savers and borrowers. In addition, financial institutions draw funds from the interbank markets and from the rediscount windows offered by central banks.

CONDITIONS AFFECTING FINANCIAL SYSTEMS

The size and strength of any financial system is the cumulative result of a large number of variables (including those discussed earlier in this chapter). Many forces work to "repress" financial markets. These forces typically include economic, social, and policy factors such as low per capita income, the political power of economic elites, currency overvaluation, excessive government spending, ineffective bank supervision, and weak or unenforced contract law.

Among economic factors, capital and money markets are often a mirror image of a country's absolute level of development since the supply and demand for capital rise with increasing incomes and production. Very few developing countries have sophisticated money and capital markets because financial system evolution is a lengthy process that tends to lag behind the development of other sectors.

The lack of effective, "formal" financial systems in developing countries creates a vacuum that is often filled by "informal" financial markets. Informal markets are those that operate outside conventional rules and institutions, and typically consist of professional and nonprofessional money lenders, extended family investment "clubs," merchants, and private pawnshops and finance firms. Informal market transactions tend to be conducted in cash to avoid official regulations and taxation. The institutional actors are usually small in scale and often enter and exit the market regularly.

Informal financial markets serve savers and borrowers who often have no access to formal institutions or instruments, often in rural but also in urban areas. Nevertheless, in comparison to formal markets, savers in informal markets tend to receive less interest and face much higher risks on their deposits. Borrowers generally pay much higher rates of interest. Therefore, both savers and borrowers ultimately benefit from the development of legal, effectively regulated financial institutions and practices.

Instability is anathema to financial system health and growth. Inflation reduces levels of confidence and spurs savers to place surplus funds in real assets (land, consumer durables, precious metals, etc.) rather than in the depreciating financial instruments. Similarly, structural balance of payments deficits lead to leakage from the local markets, in the form of both deficit financing and capital flight, because savers seek to avoid the risk of currency depreciation. The achievement of a reasonable degree of financial stability is an absolute requisite to capital market growth.

Macroeconomic policies and management exert a direct impact on financial markets. Aggregate demand management affects the general demand for funds. Monetary policies set money supply growth patterns and interest rate levels. Excessive monetary expansion adversely affects financial markets, leading to high levels of inflation and additional uncertainty and risk, especially in medium- and long-term lending practices (due to medium- and long-term interest rate uncertainty). The expansionary public investment activities taken under an irresponsible fiscal policy may crowd out productive private investment.

National legal and regulatory environments establish the parameters within which financial institutions must operate. The key variables that are derived directly from government rules and regulations include ease of entry of new firms, reserve requirements, deposit insurance structures, prudential lending requirements, credit allocation rules, financial institution supervision systems, and rules for administering insolvencies and bankruptcies.

A government's social and political objectives play a sometimes subtle but often dominant role in shaping the health and growth of financial systems. Since financial sectors lie at the center of all economic activities, governments frequently seek to maneuver capital and credit activities to meet these objectives, such as the extension of preferred credit or subsidized services to particular sectors or groups or the implicit taxation of other groups. Finally, political stability clearly plays a major role in determining levels of confidence in the economy and in financial markets.

The following sections highlight the characteristics that distinguish the economies and financial markets of developing countries from those of industrial countries (see Table 2.1).

Table 2.1
Factors Constraining Financial Market Development

FACTOR	RESULTS
Economic and Societal Factors	
Low per capita income	Low marginal savings rate
Skewed income distribution	Concentration of capital
Economic concentration in few sectors	Limits lending/investment opportunities
Inflation	Reduced incentives to save/invest in financial assets
High debts	Limits capital availability
Management inexperience in banking and other businesses	Inhibits performance of banks, reduces borrowers' ability to repay loans
Lack of real assets	Decreases accesss to funds
Family ownership	Fear loss of control
Policy Factors	
Government ownership	Reduces efficiency
Interest rate ceilings	Lowers ability of banks to attract funds, reduces savings
Excessive regulation	Decreases freedom to seek profitable loan opportunities, diversify risk
Portfolio selection restrictions	Limit investment alternative
Excessive taxation	Reduces financial returns
Budget deficits/mandated bank purchases of government paper	Drains capital from system, crowds out private sector
Barriers to entry	Subsidizes inefficient banks, limits new product development
Overvalued exchange rate	Reduces export industry returns and ability to repay loans, encourages capital flight
Weak contract law or enforcement	Precludes collections of arrearages, causes banks to require excessive collateral

Economic Variables

Any country's monetary sector is, as noted earlier, a direct reflection of the nation's "real" economy since most financial transactions involve the exchange of real goods and services. The conditions listed below typify developing country economies and financial markets. Some of the conditions can be altered in the medium term, but others can be changed only over considerable periods of time.

1. *Low levels of per capita income* result in relatively low rates of capital formation. Although numerous studies confirm that even the poorest groups in any country do save, the absolute base of income from which saving is derived is low.

2. *Skewed distributions of income and wealth* reinforce an excessive concentration of capital, encourage non-arms-length transactions, and inhibit the development of diversified sources and uses of funds.

3. *Concentrations of economic activity* in a few sectors constrain lending opportunities and increase financial system vulnerability by limiting the prospects for diversified portfolios.

4. *Chronic price instability* results in self-fulfilling inflationary expectations and in preferences for real assets, which deter capital formation.

5. *High levels of external indebtedness and chronic budget deficits* drain funds from domestic markets, give rise to periodic rescheduling crises, and reduce the new capital available for employment in productive ventures.

6. *Limited managerial and administrative capacity* within small and medium scale enterprises increases the chances for loan defaults.

7. *Lack of real assets* to serve as collateral for loans decreases entrepreneurs' access to funds and/or increases the costs of funds.

8. *Strong traditions of private/family ownership* deter small firms from raising funds through equity markets out of fear of financial disclosure or reductions in management control.

Policy Variables

Unlike economic factors, which at least in the near term must be taken as given realities, policy variables can be changed by governments. While policy frameworks are in part based on underlying economic and social conditions, they can also serve as an active catalyst for financial sector growth.

1. *Heavy direct and indirect government involvement,* intervention, and ownership constrain the private sector from participating in formal markets and from establishing financial service firms.

2. *Mandated interest rate ceilings* on deposits and loans stifle capital formation since savers often receive negative interest rates on their deposits. These ceilings also encourage investors to direct their financial assets to foreign investments to obtain higher yields than they can earn on local investments. They thereby diminish the supply of capital available for local investment.

3. *Credit allocation directives* decrease the flexibility of banks to seek profitable loan opportunities and often increase the odds for nonperforming loans. These directives are usually based upon political, social, or distributional considerations rather than on economic factors. The government is seeking to remedy what it perceives as deficiencies in the local money markets that obstruct the flow of credit at a price it considers reasonable to its priority development purposes. Allocated credit programs also require administrative burdens that most developing countries are particularly ill-equipped to handle. They also discourage savings intermediation.

4. *Portfolio selection restrictions* in secondary markets limit the range of investment alternatives available.

5. *Direct or hidden taxation* of financial transactions raises the cost of borrowing and reduces returns on capital employed. Some measures manifest themselves as implicit taxes on financial intermediaries. These controls include, *inter alia,* time limits on deposits; maximum amounts for certain deposits; and restrictions on the types of institutions that can receive certain types of deposits in the banking sector.

6. *Required purchases of government securities* force financial institutions to fund government indebtedness, often at unprofitable terms, and they crowd out private borrowers.

7. *Barriers to entry* and regulated limits to competition reinforce inefficient institutions and raise transaction costs to participants.

8. *Inappropriate exchange rate policies,* especially the maintenance of overvalued exchange rates, lead to distorted lending decisions, financial remittance restrictions, and increased capital flight. Conversely, these price distortions serve as a disincentive for domestic savings mobilization.

9. *Inefficient, cumbersome legal systems* make contract enforcement difficult and seriously impede efforts by financial institutions to collect overdue loan payments.

Resulting Financial Market Conditions

The factors and policies described above are not present in every developing country, nor are they limited to developing countries. However, more often than not they represent a reasonably accurate picture of operational characteristics of money and capital markets in those nations. The end result of these and related variables is what some financial analysts have termed "financial repression," or the externally-imposed restriction of the financial sector in providing services for savings, investment, and borrowing.

If a given system is permitted to operate according to market principles and conditions, the only major consequence of economic underdevelopment is the delay of the natural evolution toward a modern financial system. However, when inappropriate policy stances are added to low development levels, the result is an abnormal evolution of the financial sector. It is characterized by seemingly intractable and mutually reinforcing constraints. The most common attributes of such systems are as follows:

- Formal capital markets are "thin and narrow," and possess only limited capital for use by productive enterprises.
- Levels of capital stock remain low, and rates of capital formation are negligible.
- Interest rate ceilings reduce the incentive to save and artificially inflate prices of real assets.
- Borrowers remain heavily dependent on short-term rollover financing to cover both their credit and capital requirements.
- Small-scale and medium-scale firms have limited access to financial credit, leading to the development of informal or curb markets and raising the cost of funds to borrowers.
- Limited options and instruments for savers create excessive demand for existing instruments, driving down their returns.
- Borrowers unable to gain access to local funds seek foreign sources of funds unless they are restricted.
- The transaction costs of financial institutions remain high due to inefficiency and lack of flexibility.
- Formal markets are dominated by concentrated lending portfolios, with many credits extended by government directive to large industrial and/or government-owned firms.
- The profitability of unsubsidized sectors (often agriculture) is reduced by implicit taxation imposed through financial transactions.
- Domestically-produced savings are lost through capital flight.
- Negative real interest rates, particularly for "preferred" borrowers in the formal sector, give rise to excessively capital-intensive production methods and operating inefficiencies.

- Since inefficient legal systems often deter lenders from taking recourse on loan defaults, lenders require abnormally high collateral for borrowings.

The policy strategies that have created the conditions noted above are often attempts to achieve political, social, and economic goals. For example, interest rate ceilings have long been considered an appropriate means to stem inflationary pressures and prevent usurious lending rates. Nevertheless, the introduction of one form of control almost always necessitates another. Interest rate ceilings, for example, give rise to the need for credit allocation controls because demand for funds will inevitably outstrip their supply.

The ultimate consequence is the erection of a make-shift system of controls and counter-controls, the combination of which introduces a host of distortions and above all a set of serious disincentives to capital formation. While each policy intervention creates a new set of "winners" and "losers," the final cost—retardation of financial market development—is borne by all participants in the economy.

Liberalizing financial markets through the dismantling of restrictions and unwarranted controls reintroduces incentives for households and firms to save and invest surplus funds in financial instruments, and for borrowers to seek capital and credit to employ for productive purposes. The efficient use of capital in turn raises overall economic activity, thereby generating needed jobs, exports, and foreign exchange. The increase in the overall capital stock generated by reforms permits higher rates of growth and standards of living.

3 The Public/Private Debate

Government involvement in financial markets can range from a heavy direct role to one in which governments simply oversee the activities of private sector institutions. This chapter addresses the relative efficiency of public and private financial intermediaries.

GOVERNMENT OWNERSHIP OF FINANCIAL INTERMEDIARIES

Developing country financial systems are composed of a variety of financial intermediaries, as noted in Chapter 2. Ownership varies from country to country, with an array of public and private intermediaries participating in these systems. There are few banking functions, however, that are exclusive to the public or private sector (with the exception of public functions such as printing money). For example, governments and donors relied on public development banks and development finance institutions to channel funds to small enterprises in developing countries until the early 1980s. Donors began to rely increasingly on private development banks to deliver services in the 1980s (which, by the way, outperformed their public sector counterparts). With the exception of "government participants," the financial intermediaries discussed in the preceding chapter could be found in the public or private sector.

Most developing country financial systems are mixed, with both public and private financial institutions, foreign and domestic. The mix of ownership ranges from total public ownership and control to a mixed (public and private) formal system to an informal financial system. The most common form of publicly-owned financial institution in developing countries is the nationalized financial intermediary.

The governments of many developing countries have nationalized major components of the commercial banking system in order to eliminate foreign control and make the commercial banking system more responsive to public policy. In some countries virtually all the banks are government owned and operated.

Nationalization of financial institutions has often been undertaken in the Third World because of the critical importance of banks to the economy. Examples of major nationalizations include the 1987 bank takeover in Peru by the Garcia government, the nationalization of the banks in Chile under Allende, and the nationalization of the entire banking sector in El Salvador in 1979 to support agrarian reform under the Duarte administration. In Africa, nationalized banking systems are found in Angola, Mozambique, and Tanzania. Nationalizations are often politically popular and are more easily accomplished than privatizations.

Bank nationalizations have been undertaken because a nationalized banking sector can be ordered by the government to allocate credit among selected, priority economic activities and to provide long-term loans to preferred sectors. This motivation was the case in El Salvador, where each nationalized bank was directed to provide working capital to land reform cooperatives. Thus, the nationalized banking sector often becomes an instrument for carrying out the political agenda of the government.

Furthermore, governments can gain popular support by portraying nationalization as a means to direct funds away from business elites who may control a country's economic machinery. Other governments have nationalized foreign banking operations in order to capture the perceived excess rents of those operations. Whatever the political motivation, bank nationalizations tend to stay in place, at least until economic conditions deteriorate to the point where privatization or de-nationalization becomes inevitable.

Similarly, a government bank may serve as a conduit for subsidies to certain economic activities. This process is often reinforced because the recipients of the subsidies form effective constituencies to further their interests. The disruptions caused in the rural economy of New Zealand when the Rural Bank was compelled to charge market interest rates, and the subsequent pressure from agricultural sector businesses, provide a good example of why governments hesitate to tamper with existing subsidies or with the channels through which they are directed.

Government officials also use public ownership of financial institutions for personal financial gain. This was the case in the Philippines, where President Marcos used two government-owned lending institutions, the Philippine National Bank and the Development Bank of the Philippines, to channel massive amounts of credit to corporations set up by his associates. Many of these corporations had limited commercial viability, but the lending mechanism served to enrich both Marcos and his associates. Until the Marcos government fell in early 1986, little if any thought was given to the possibility of privatizing these banks. When the Aquino government took office, these two major state-owned banks were overburdened with non-performing assets that contributed to the country's financial crisis. This led to the divestiture of the non-performing assets as a major component in that privatization program. (See Appendix A for more on the Philippines.)

PUBLIC VERSUS PRIVATE SECTOR PERFORMANCE

Ownership matters. The incentives extended to individuals and organizations, and the goals and procedures that are adopted by them, are a function of top management decisions and/or ownership discretion and control. If ownership is separated from management, as it often is the case in modern societies, then management takes its cues from the owners.

Owners play a dominant role in business operations. They determine, directly or indirectly, who is hired, what goods and services are produced, how they are distributed, what prices are charged, and what is an acceptable profit level. Applying these to banking, one finds that bank ownership plays a determinant role in personnel staffing levels and qualifications, the mix and distribution of savings and credit instruments, the locations of branch banks, and the interest levels paid and charged.

A major explanation behind the performance differences between private and state-owned financial institutions is property rights theory. Numerous studies demonstrate the differences resulting from a particular type of ownership (i.e., private versus public), although few analyses have looked at these differences in banks and other financial institutions.

A 1981 study examined economic behavior in the private and government banks in Australia's banking system.[1] Comparing banks with similar characteristics, other than ownership, this study arrived at four interesting conclusions. First, managers of government-owned banks hold a higher proportion of their bank's assets in low-risk and low-paying investments than do their private counterparts. Second, managers of government-owned banks arrange their banks' affairs so that they have easier, less arduous lives. Also, government-owned banks grow more rapidly and have larger staffs than privately-owned banks. Finally, public managers monitor and organize work and workers less effectively than do private managers. The result of these four conclusions is reflected in the substantially lower profit rates experienced in the public sector. Similarly, the rate of return on "sales" and the rate of return on capital are significantly higher for private than for government firms.

Privately-owned banks differ significantly from government-owned banks in many regards. Some of the more important variances are described below. Throughout this paper, government-owned banks are defined as banks owned 50 percent or more by one or more government entities, whether local, regional, or national.

Bank Administration

Privately-owned banks have generally operated more efficiently and profitably than those owned by the government. The higher efficiency is a result of incentives for bank personnel and management to keep costs low and revenues and profits high. Faced with higher costs of capital than those offered to their public sector counterparts, private owners of banks focus on "the bottom line." They also enforce stricter accounting and reporting standards for their clients, which increases the level of integrity in the financial system and investor confidence.

In contrast, government owners do not report to profit-seeking stock-holders and often do not even publish the equivalent of profit and loss statements or annual reports. Secure in their jobs, government workers do not face the same pressures to work rapidly and accurately as do private sector employees who do not enjoy a similar degree of job security.

The limited quantitative information that is available supports the conclusion that private sector banks are more efficient. Table 3.1 illustrates the relative administrative efficiency of seventeen development banks around the world, eight of which are government-owned and nine of which are privately-owned. In most cases, private development banks out-perform state-owned institutions in the same country. In both Ecuador and Korea, privately-owned banks incur lower administrative expenses relative to total assets than do their government-owned counterparts. The private development bank in Ecuador was 26 percent more efficient than the state-owned bank, while the private institution in Korea was 133 percent more efficient, on average, than the government-owned banks.

Table 3.1

A Quantitative Comparison of Government and Privately Owned Development Banks

Country and Institution	Admin. Expenses as % of Assets	Gross Income as % of Assets	Financial Expenses as % of Assets
East Africa			
Public DFCs			
BDC/Botswana	4.1	13.0	5.3
TIB/Tanzania	1.0	7.4	2.5
Average, Public DFCs	2.6	10.2	3.9
Private DFCs			
SOFIDE/Zaire	6.3	12.2	3.8
West Africa			
Private DFCs			
SOFISEDIT/Senegal	5.0	9.6	8.1
Latin America & Caribbean			
Public DFCs			
CFN/Ecuador	2.4	9.0	6.4
Private DFCs			
COFIEC/Ecuador	1.9	.9.0	3.9
East Asia & Pacific			
Public DFCs			
BAPINDO/Indonesia	3.7	12.5	7.4
DBP/Philippines	1.4	7.3	6.7
CNB/Korea	4.2	14.6	9.5
KDB/Korea	0.9	10.6	7.4
SMIB/Korea	3.5	12.3	8.6
Avg., Korean Public DFCs	2.4	11.7	8.0
Average, Public DFCs	2.5	10.9	7.6
Private DFCs			
DBS/Singapore	1.3	8.9	5.9
KDFC-KLB/Korea	1.0	11.8	8.1
PDCP/Philippines	1.8	12.6	7.4
PISO/Philippines	2.7	9.1	3.4
PDFCI/Indonesia	3.7	12.7	6.8
Average, Private DFCs	2.1	11.0	6.3
South Asia			
Private DFCs			
PICIC/Pakistan	0.7	9.2	6.6
Worldwide			
Average, Public DFCs	2.3	9.6	5.9
Average, Private DFCs	2.2	9.7	5.7

Source: World Bank, "DFCs: State and Privately Owned," Staff Working Paper No. 578, 1983. All figures are averages for 1977 - 1979.

In the East Asia and the Pacific region, privately-run development banks incurred on average only 80 percent of the administrative costs of government-owned institutions to handle a given asset level. Private banks worldwide averaged lower administrative costs than their public sector counterparts. It is interesting to note that private banks demonstrate lower administrative costs per unit of assets even given the likelihood that private sector employees are paid more than public sector workers.

Governments have not historically been concerned with the internal efficiency of state-owned enterprises (SOEs). That attitude has been changing recently, however, as governments have become aware of the large budget pressures that result from propping up inefficient SOEs.

In the particular case of banks, there is an additional reason for government concern. Administrative costs and profits are, in simple terms, a part of the differential between interest rates paid to savers and those charged to borrowers. To the extent that governments can set a framework (i.e., private banking) in which administrative costs are low, rates paid on savings can rise, encouraging additional saving and releasing new resources for growth. Similarly, borrowing rates can fall, lowering the cost of doing business and spurring investment and economic development.

Resource Mobilization

To improve their chances for self-sustaining viability, financial institutions need to mobilize funds from the domestic economy. Whether public or private, banks look primarily to four sources for funds to lend: domestic savers, the government, international capital sources such as private banks and multilateral development banks, and paid-in capital and retained earnings. Although the record for mobilizing domestic resources is generally poor for both private and state-owned intermediate financial institutions, the available evidence shows that private banks perform better in this important respect.

Private financial institutions have been more efficient than public institutions at mobilizing domestic resources in support of financial markets. Because of their more limited access to concessionary resources, they have to depend to a greater extent on their capacity to attract nonconcessionary savings and to engage in new financial activities. Accordingly, they have been more active in exploiting new opportunities in merchant banking, brokerage, money markets, etc.

Government-owned banks tend to rely heavily on funds from their central bank or national treasury and from multilateral development banks (often made available at highly subsidized rates). They largely ignore the resources available in the local capital market. Since the treasury ultimately guarantees the solvency of public institutions, their need for additional capital to offset the erosion of their capital base by inflation is less urgent than it is for private banks. Similarly, public banks that can count on continued donor support on concessional terms have little incentive to search for capital from private domestic sources. In contrast, private lending institutions with no other options open to them have strong incentives for competing for private funds on commercial terms to increase their capital base.

There are many instances where public banks have been found to possess greater potential for amassing capital than private institutions. However, these situations often reflect the national government's desire to reinvigorate traditional industrial, agricultural, or mining projects.

Once banks are privatized, there is often a surge of resource mobilization and financial deepening as increased confidence in the banking system and more attractive savings instruments attract new funds from savers. Thus, state-owned banks often repress the evolution of viable local sources of capital and contribute to capital flight. Private banks, denied easy access to government subsidies, are generally more effective at mobilizing local resources.

Several case study examples illustrate this point. The barely functioning state-owned banks in Guinea attracted very few deposits and operated instead as channels for subsidized government credit. Following the implementation of privatization and financial reform in the mid-1980s, resource mobilization improved somewhat. However, negative real interest rates for savers, a result of government interest rate ceilings and high inflation, have kept local savings low.

Results have been better where financial reforms have allowed interest rates to rise to encourage savings. Chile saw a rise in the most widely used financial deepening indicator (the ratio of M2, a broad monetary aggregate, to GDP), from 15 percent to 48 percent in the decade following privatization and reform. In Bangladesh, this indicator of financial deepening grew from 20 percent to 25 percent in the seven years following financial sector privatization and liberalization.

The differential between the ability and predisposition of government versus private banks to mobilize local savings points to an important conclusion. By invigorating local sources of capital, private banks tend to reduce the need for local financial markets to depend on foreign borrowing. The protracted debt crisis being experienced throughout the developing world provides an additional impetus for privatization.

Product Development and Diversification

In their quest to attract and retain clients, private banks aggressively use one of the most powerful tools open to them: the innovation and dissemination of new banking products. Examples of new products include instruments for both savers and borrowers, such as certificates of deposit, interest bearing checking accounts, foreign currency accounts, and instruments denominated in real terms. Private banks are more likely to be creative in developing and gaining approval for new banking products because they depend more heavily than public sector banks on local depositors for funds. The increased use of new products also provides private banks with an advantage over public banks in reducing transaction costs and spreading out the costs of bearing risks. The predominance of public sector banks in developing countries is thought to be one reason why the financial markets in those nations have not developed the wide range of instruments available in other countries.

In most goods markets, the government is and should be unconcerned with the range of products available. This indifference is not the case, however, in financial markets because of the economy-wide benefits associated with savings. Side-effects (either positive or negative) of production or consumption that affect people other than direct producers or consumers are called "externalities." Savings generates positive externalities. Savings create capital, which can be productively invested to expand output, jobs, exports, and foreign exchange. Thus, private banks' tendency to create new instruments and increase savings leads ultimately to greater production and more jobs. Conversely, the negative effects of the government-owned banks' failure to create attractive savings instruments and mobilize local savings reverberate through the economy.

Diversification allows institutions to overcome the problems of scale associated with over-specialization, especially in low-income countries with small financial markets. State-owned banks are generally less prone than private banks to diversify because they tend to look to governments or donors, not private investors, to replenish their capital as needed. They also generally stick to their assigned function in lending for designated priority sectors, small sector enterprises, or export financing.

Credit Allocation

Government and private banks also differ in the criteria they use to allocate credit. Private banks tend to use creditworthiness as the deciding criterion, whereas politically driven allocations are prevalent in some state-owned institutions. Government institutions are more likely to approve credit according to some predetermined formula, for example, 30 percent of the portfolio to agriculture, 40 percent to heavy industry, etc. This difference between public and private allocations stems from the fundamentally different incentives under which the banks operate. Government officials are more likely to respond to pressure from other officials and agencies because in some cases their jobs depend on maintaining good relations. In addition, neither individual transactions nor the overall bank performance will be monitored carefully for profitability.

In contrast, private bank officials are held accountable for the outcome of the loans they approve. The future of their careers and the bank itself depends on lending funds to projects that generate a profit and repay the loan and interest on time. Private banks allocate credit based on expected profitability because of the ownership structure and the demands that owners place on the entire bank organization. Private banks have greatly improved the local standards of project appraisal, selection, and follow-up. Thus, credit is more likely to be channelled to those projects with high rates of return in a system in which funds are intermediated by private banks rather than in a system dominated by state-owned banks.

The closeness of the public financial institution to the rest of the government may make it more vulnerable to political decisions and may limit its capacity to apply objective criteria in project evaluation. Public banks have closer access to key decision makers in the public sector and have a greater capacity to bargain within the government in favor of their own objectives.

Although private financial institutions are somewhat better able to avoid government-sponsored programs and projects of dubious profitability than are public ones, private ownership or control in itself cannot guarantee against government pressures to fund unprofitable projects. If powerful officials seek particular loan approvals or other decisions—whether from political or personal motives—the private financial institution may find it hard to resist.

Loan Collection

Private banks appear to be more efficient than their public counterparts in handling loans. The same pressures that encourage private institutions to make lending decisions based on financial and cash flow analyses also push them to collect loans vigorously. The emphasis on the "bottom-line," the careful tracking of loans and financial performance, and the strong link between individual careers and loan performance all act as incentives for vigilant loan collection efforts.

In contrast, these incentives are often absent in state-owned banks. In an environment where career progression is tied more closely to political connections than to loan decisions and performance, bad loans are less likely to receive close attention and monitoring and less likely to be the subject of vigorous enforcement.

The lack of effective loan collections has deleterious effects not only on the individual banks that must take the write-offs but also on the entire financial system. Loans come to be regarded more as gifts than contracts that must be fulfilled. The government banks that allow non-payers to escape their commitments, and even receive additional credit, create an atmosphere in which bad debt rates, and therefore the costs of contract enforcement, rise throughout the financial system.

Personnel Recruitment, Supervision and Compensation

In banking, as in all service industries, staff quality is a key to success because personnel is the principal input from which banking services are generated. The right individual with the right skills can make the difference between keeping and losing a client and between distinguishing a profitable loan from an unprofitable one.

Public sector banks labor under a number of personnel restrictions and requirements to which private banks are not subject. Government-owned institutions are often pressured to hire individuals based more on connections than competence. Lower salary scales often discourage more experienced individuals from accepting public sector jobs. Overstaffing in government-owned banks is widespread since public sector managers are rewarded more for controlling large bureaucracies than for efficiently using staff to perform given functions. Staff review, evaluation and supervision are often almost perfunctory. Employment and promotions are less a function of individual output and more a function of political pressure.

In contrast, private banks are able to attract and hold personnel, especially managers, of superior ability. Private banks generally have more discretion than public banks in personnel actions regarding the number of employees, hiring and firing, and the enforcement of work discipline. Private banks hire, supervise, promote, and release staff based on their perceived ability to add to the bank's fundamental goal of providing quality service to clients in order to earn a profit. While contacts and connections still matter, they usually matter less. Private enterprises more closely resemble meritocracies than do public firms. Staffing levels in private banks are likely to be much lower than those in government institutions. Indeed, disposing of excess personnel is one of the most troublesome issues encountered in privatizations.

NOTE

1. David G. Davies, "Property Rights and Economic Behavior in Private and Government Enterprises: The Case of Australia's Banking System," *Research in Law and Economics*, Vol. 3, 1981. The findings of this paper were recently updated and reconfirmed in an unpublished paper by Peter F. Brucato Jr. and David G. Davies, "Property Rights, Managerial Behavior, and Firm Performance: A Study of Government and Privately-Owned Banks in Australia," 1990.

4 Understanding Financial Sector Liberalization

Financial sector liberalization, or the movement from current repressed conditions to a deregulated, competitive, appropriately-supervised system, should proceed along two vectors—the achievement of financial stability through the adoption of appropriate monetary and fiscal policies and the deregulation of the financial system itself. At one level, instability and excessive regulation feed upon themselves and result in a closed cycle of financial repression. The dynamics of this relationship are that conditions of chronic instability lead to a desire by or requirement for the government to erect increasingly rigid controls over the financial system. These controls in turn reduce the flexibility and resources needed by economic units to carry out their functions, which ultimately constrains the economy from overcoming the root causes of instability.

At a second level, one which is more visible to policymakers, instability and regulation are viewed as opposite ends of a continuum. That is, excessive deregulation of financial markets leads to instability. Therefore, governments are loathe to reduce their control over financial variables as long as the symptoms of instability persist.

The actual experience of developing and developed countries alike confirms that the first critical task in any financial reform strategy is to secure some semblance of financial stability. Instability reduces confidence in currencies and induces market participants to avoid formal systems of exchange. The important processes of saving, borrowing, and intermediating funds are complicated, sometimes to the point where "normal" transactions are effectively eliminated.

In recent years, a marked distinction has been drawn between the sustained growth performance of many East and Southeast Asian nations on the one hand and the generalized economic stagnation of many Central and South American countries on the other. The key determinant underlying this differential has been that the former countries undertook concerted efforts to achieve financial stability as a basis for long-term growth, whereas the latter nations became mired in a continuous, downward cycle of financial instability and external indebtedness. The lesson one can draw is that governments are advised to take whatever difficult steps are necessary to achieve financial stability.

FINANCIAL STABILITY

Political stability is necessary for financial markets to function efficiently. Stability contributes to confidence that public policies favorable to economic growth and the development of a competitive private sector will be sustained. Such a situation is necessary to encourage the long-term commitment required for viable financial systems.

Financial instability inhibits prospective savers from relying on the formal financial system. Instead, they hold more traditional forms of wealth such as land, animals, jewelry, or gold. The result is an aggregate level of savings less than that which could be achieved given improved financial markets policies. Inadequate information, distrust of large and centralized institutions, and various cultural considerations are other factors that inhibit savers from relying more fully on formal financial markets.

People with sufficient income to save will not invest in insecure financial markets. Under such circumstance, the tendency is for savings to be invested in other (developed) countries, gold, real estate, or other investments. Financial volatility has been a major deterrent to economic growth in many developing countries. In the absence of stability, available surpluses either are invested in relatively nonproductive assets or are leaked from the economy in the form of flight capital.

The principal characteristics of financial instability are high levels of inflation, structural government budget and balance of payments deficits, currency volatility and debasement, and chronic capital flight. Each of these conditions is anathema to domestic capital formation. The ultimate elimination of instability can only be achieved through the bitter medicine of "structural adjustment" measures—various policies to reduce excessive government and private consumption.

In most countries the key problem is government excess. Governments simply spend more than they earn in revenues. To meet their financing needs, governments force the purchase of their securities, raise reserve requirements and mandatory deposit levels with government agencies, exploit seigniorage rights by printing new currency and expanding the money supply, and borrow from international capital and credit markets. Seigniorage is the revenue earned by governments through additions in the supply of currency.

Other sources of instability include the maintenance of trade and foreign exchange policies that reduce competitiveness, the imposition of price controls, and the extension of subsidies and other programs that distort prices and output. Unfortunately, each of these practices becomes ingrained over time in the policy structure, develops its own set of beneficiaries, and is extremely difficult to eliminate.

As any national leadership can attest, there are no simple solutions to the problem of financial instability. Each curative measure incurs costs that governments or their constituents are reluctant to bear. However, a standard set of policies that has proved successful in achieving stability includes the following courses of action.

Reduce and Improve Effectiveness of Government Expenditures

Over time, governments must seek to "balance their books" by reducing spending. This goal implies the need to reduce both capital and recurrent expenditures through the reduction or elimination of existing programs and projects. In addition, expenditures should be shifted to areas of highest social return and away from inefficient "pork-barrel" projects.

As difficult as they may seem in practice, efforts to balance budgets through expenditure curbs yield at least two important benefits for financial markets. First, they reduce inflationary pressures caused by deficit spending stimulus. Second, they decrease the phenomenon of "crowding out," in which governments absorb the majority of liquidity in the system and lower the access of private enterprises to capital and credit.

Increase Government Revenues

In addition to cutting expenditures, government authorities often need to seek new sources of tax revenue. In many cases tax collection systems can be improved to capture higher percentages of direct taxes incurred but not paid.

Governments willing to examine all potential sources of revenue will generally find numerous opportunities. Government enterprises or privileged sectors are often "free riders" and should pay taxes. Import quotas can be changed to tariff systems. Registration systems (real estate transfers, financial transactions, company incorporation, etc.) can generate fees. These and other measures can provide additional revenue streams to finance government operations.

Modernize the Tax System

In some countries, tax measures inhibit financial market development and restrict capital formation by increasing the cost of financial intermediation and reducing the financial system's flexibility. They reduce the funds available for lending and, in turn, for investing. Stability is best achieved by broadening the tax base, preferably shifting toward direct taxation and removing tax-driven subsidies and disincentives. Tax reforms should also eliminate biases in favor of debt financing and against equity financing and the use of other secondary market instruments.

Financial intermediation is subject to explicit and implicit tax measures that are not applied to other sectors of the economy. For example, some governments impose an explicit transactions tax on the value of each financial transaction undertaken by a financial institution. Implicit taxes consist primarily of requirements for the maintenance of high reserve levels and forced portfolio investments in low-yielding government securities.

Many developing countries operate tax regimes that are onerous or even confiscatory on paper, but are largely ignored or poorly enforced. In these instances, an appropriate strategy would be to reduce tax rates to reasonable levels and take appropriate steps to improve collection. A key ingredient in the development of modern economic sectors is increasing acceptance of rational rather than excessive rules and procedures. Also important is the gradual removal of fraud and corruption from the system. These efforts will involve substantial policy debate as financial market development may conflict with other government goals, such as raising short-term tax revenue.

Maintain Positive Real Interest Rates

The conventional wisdom of the past was that interest rate ceilings were needed to contain inflationary pressures. The actual experience of success cases such as Taiwan, Chile, Turkey and others proves the opposite, that rates reflecting the true cost and value of money (i.e., relatively high rates) lead to the suppression of inflation and equally important to a more efficient allocation of financial resources.

Unless interest rates exceed rates of inflation, conditions encourage investors to speculate in real estate and tradeable commodities rather than to invest in productive investments. Without a positive return on local financial assets, investors try to hold their assets overseas where returns are higher, which leads to capital flight. In general, developing countries should have higher real interest rates than developed countries to attract needed capital and compensate for generally higher political, financial, and legal risks.

Negative real interest rates constitute a subsidy on capital and hence create incentives for excessively capital-intensive forms of production. If industries become dependent on cheap money to finance their capital expansions and current operations, they become vulnerable in periods of rising real costs of funds. However, the potential for bankruptcies and resulting economic losses should not be used as a permanent excuse for inaction; entire economies pay the price for ongoing credit subsidies.

Countries that have consistently maintained positive interest rates and have an adequate number of institutions that issue attractive financial instruments show a higher rate of growth in their financial assets and have deeper financial intermediary systems than countries that have low and/or widely fluctuating levels of real interest on deposits. Positive market-determined real interest rates generally are associated with the development of sound and self-sustaining financial systems. The results of strategies in which national authorities shifted from negative to positive real interest rates within a rational overall plan has been uniformly good. Inflation subsided, financial markets stabilized, capital flight declined, and increasing amounts of saving entered the banking system.

Control Money Supply Growth

Many governments resort to printing money in order to meet government obligations. In addition, policymakers often maintain low reserve requirements in efforts to provide economic stimulus. If continued over time, these practices cause chronic inflationary pressures.

Financial instability is combatted by restricting the expansion of monetary aggregates. Seigniorage should be used as only a limited source for government revenues. Restricting the growth of the money supply is typically the appropriate means to raise interest rates.

Maintain Competitive Exchange Rates

Exchange rates must be at competitive levels to discourage capital flight and to encourage exports and domestic production. The typical condition in countries with repressed financial systems is currency overvaluation, which *ceteris paribus* provides an incentive to import and a disincentive to export.

The standard prescription in this case is currency devaluation coupled with tightened monetary policy to stem the inflationary impact of depreciation. The latter sends a signal that further large-scale devaluations are not expected. In addition, an exchange rate policy that maintains a competitive rate by adjusting it for inflation levels should be implemented. For many developing countries, the shallowness of capital markets makes a completely free-market rate policy an undesirable policy.

Remove Price Controls

Price controls are seen as an expedient method to contain inflation in the short run, but inevitably they are ineffective and in many cases actually stimulate price rises. They act to reduce the availability of supply and ultimately reduce production. Therefore, the gradual elimination of controls is often an important component of stabilization strategies.

Corollary Policy Reforms

Most economic stabilization programs include some combination of the policies described above. Other policy reforms aim at stimulating economic activity and efficiency. These include shifting from quantitative import restrictions to tariffs and reducing duties on needed inputs and raw materials; eliminating export taxes and other disincentives to exporters; establishing tax or other incentives for new investment; and reducing bureaucratic "red tape."

Sequence Reforms Appropriately

The sequencing of financial and macroeconomic reforms is critically important. A large body of literature focuses on whether capital controls should be eased before or after trade controls. Exact sequencing depends on many factors, some of which are unique to individual countries. As a result, the academic and policy communities admit that proper sequencing is not yet fully understood.

The general consensus among policymakers and economists is that basic macroeconomic reforms should be adopted first. Later, controls on the flow of goods and money across borders should be removed. Specifically, the first priority should be placed on introducing and then maintaining competitive exchange rates and positive real interest rates. Then, trade policies should be liberalized and, finally, controls on capital flows should be eased.

One reason for liberalizing trade policies before lifting capital controls is that any inappropriate changes can be reversed or modified before large quantities of real resources are affected. Because of the speed at which money can be moved, the response to adjustments in capital controls is likely to be sudden and large. Millions of dollars in foreign or local currency can cross borders overnight. The rapid transfer of large volumes of funds can greatly increase the cost of inappropriate adjustments. In contrast, investor response to changes in tariffs and exchange rates are much slower. A longer time lag is required to make a real investment as opposed to a portfolio investment. Similarly, changes in goods flows (trade) are also inherently slower because of transportation delays and limited consumption demand.

In addition, the adjustment process is much smoother if trade controls are lifted prior to capital controls. Once trade barriers are lifted, real investment based on a non-distorted assessment of the profitability of alternative projects can commence. Assuming capital controls have not been lifted, portfolio investment will continue to be based on distorted incentives. When restrictions on the capital accounts of the balance of payments are subsequently lifted, portfolio investment (but not real investment) will have to adjust. Because of its nature, the adjustment will be fairly rapid.

BANKING SYSTEM DEREGULATION

Financial regulation and supervision consists of the policies and rules established to govern the operations of participating institutions and to direct the development of money and capital markets. Certain policies such as reserve requirements and interest rate controls are both instruments of economic policy and means to regulate the behavior of financial institutions.

Debates regarding what constitutes an "appropriate" degree of financial system regulation, as opposed to excessive or insufficient regulation, have been carried on for decades and centuries without resolution. However, historical experience has indicated conclusively that inadequate regulation and supervision lead to financial instability and crisis. Excessive regulation, on the other hand, impedes capital formation and constrains the ability of the financial markets to contribute to economic development. The only available option is, therefore, to put into place a system that represents a working compromise between the two extremes.

The financial systems of most developing countries are subject to greater regulation than are their counterparts in industrial countries. Developing country governments generally seek to exert greater control over the economy as a whole, and the financial sector plays a key role in the exercise of control. In many developing countries, the integrity and enforcement of legal codes and regulations are often inadequate on such issues as security of assets, title to property, property transfer, taking possession of collateral on loans in default, and sharing ownership of assets. The result is that under existing laws, it is often difficult to broaden the range of financial instruments and securities available in the market. There are also limits on when and at what price companies can issue securities in public offerings (inhibiting public offerings). In addition, government leaders feel their capital and money markets are not well developed, and hence are more vulnerable to external shocks. In certain cases, private market actors in developing countries are deemed as more likely to engage in fraudulent practices.

Over the past decade, development policy practitioners have reached the conclusion that over-regulation can actually prove counterproductive to the attainment of stability and accelerated growth. This view has been reinforced by the general deregulation movement experienced in industrial countries in recent years. As a result, financial market deregulation has been set in motion in many nations. Responsible regulation of private banking and other financial institutions may remove some of the host government's excuses for nationalization of financial institutions and resistance to privatization of state-owned financial institutions. Policymakers and regulators are normally presented with the following "portfolio" of reform possibilities.

Remove Interest Rate Ceilings on Certain Classes of Deposits or Loans

Interest rates represent the cost of funds to holders and users and therefore are the most powerful determinant of saving and borrowing. Ceilings often result in negative real rates of interest, which deter saving and encourage borrowing. The removal of such ceilings reduces or eliminates these biases against capital market deepening. Interest rate ceilings often are imposed by governments to protect the borrower from "unscrupulous" lending practices. Yet, lending to large numbers of small and widely dispersed borrowers (e.g., small, rural entrepreneurs) normally involves relatively high administrative costs per loan that cannot be passed on to the end-borrower because of the interest rate ceiling. Consequently, it becomes unprofitable for financial institutions to lend to these borrowers.

Imposing interest rate ceilings, no matter how well-intentioned, often results in reductions, not increases, in the availability of formal credit for specific target groups. Local financial institutions handling the subsidized credit can be expected to allocate the funds in accordance with their appraisal of risk and profitability for themselves. They may improve the quality but not expand the dispersion of their loans. Thus, it seems likely that the largest, most prosperous, and most creditworthy borrowers will be given priority over the low-income borrowers that the government may have intended to be the beneficiaries of the cheap credit.

Decrease or Abolish Barriers to Entry by Private Domestic and/or Foreign Banks

Many financial systems are essentially closed to new entrants, which in effect protects existing firms from competition and allows them to operate inefficiently. Through the provision of market access to new banks, competitive forces are introduced and market participants can turn to new sources for funds and financial services. Competition in banking and financial intermediation tends to limit the spreads between the interest paid by borrowers and that received by depositors. Narrowing this spread is an incentive for increasing saving and provides more funds, more cheaply, to investors. Competition, when combined with the adoption of other liberalized financial sector reforms, enhances the efficiency with which intermediation is performed. The reduction of entry barriers in Chile, the Philippines, and Turkey strengthened the banking system in those countries.

Reduce Excessive Reserve Requirements

Reserve requirements are employed for reasons of controlling money supply growth and assuring the capital adequacy of banks. Excessive reserve requirements or mandatory deposits with government agencies, however, are often imposed for the thinly veiled purpose of financing government deficits. High reserve requirements reduce the flow of funds to productive enterprises as well as decrease bank profitability.

Eliminate Unreasonable Portfolio Allocation Rules

Financial institutions are required to meet certain guidelines concerning their investments (in loans or financial instruments) in order to protect the security of their depositors' assets. However, regulations may require that loan portfolio shares be maintained for "priority" sectors, without regard to profitability and risk, or that extremely high proportions of financial portfolios be held in the form of government instruments. The prudent relaxation of these rules will release capital for use by private businesses.

Administrative credit allocation mechanisms are particularly appealing to very low income countries where money markets are typically shallow and fragmented between geographic regions, urban and rural borrowers, different loan purposes, large and small enterprises, and classes of borrowers. Often, developing country governments understandably want to ensure access to scarce loan resources for investments that they believe promise high yields in economic development terms but are unattractive to private financial institutions because of their high risks and low financial yields. Over-reliance on measures that direct credit contrary to market forces can result in misallocation of scarce investment resources, undermining the strength and viability of credit institutions and retarding the growth of financial assets.

Shift Emphasis from Regulation to Supervision

Many developing countries and certain industrial countries are "long" on regulation and "short" on supervision. One reason is that it is easier to tell institutions how to behave than to monitor their actual behavior. A general movement to improve the quality and capabilities of bank examiners would reduce the need for what often are considered "nuisance" regulations.

Standardize Reporting Guidelines and Require Adequate Financial Audits of Banks and Nonfinancial Companies

Very often excessive regulation is seen as an antidote to the lack of proper financial reporting by banking and nonbanking firms. Much of this problem could be addressed by a movement toward transparency and public access to financial records.

Allow Unprofitable Banks to Fail, but Protect at Least Small Depositors

A major dilemma facing all bank regulators is the decision to permit financial institutions to fail. While absolute receiverships can normally be avoided through mergers and acquisitions, the prospects of possible bankruptcies send strong messages to depositors and lethargic bank management.

Encourage Self Regulation

Self regulation is a novel concept in many societies; but it can, over time, preclude the need for strong governmental controls with all of their negative side-effects. Bankers associations, for example, can develop oversight capabilities to police their members' behavior. In addition, the presence of private credit or paper rating agencies provide useful information to investors and depositors.

Authorize Banks to Engage in Broader Ranges of Financial Services

In many countries, banks are constrained in their liberty to offer new financial instruments or services. This restriction limits their growth potential and their ability to seek new profit opportunities. Reducing the lines drawn between different financial subsectors can act as a powerful motive to increase efficiency through the introduction of competitive forces.

OPERATIONAL GUIDELINES AND PRINCIPLES

The basic premise underlying this analysis is that appropriate financial market reforms as well as privatization of financial institutions can remove important constraints and act as powerful stimulants to private sector-led growth. Recognize, however, that reform initiatives require careful planning and execution to preclude undesired consequences and instabilities. No segment of any economy is more potentially volatile than the financial system since funds can in most cases be shifted with great speed and ease. Therefore, the adoption and use of certain procedural guidelines can enhance the prospects for successful policy development and implementation.

Approach Financial Policy Reform as a Means to an End Rather than an End in Itself

Capital and money markets exist for the purpose of assisting individuals and firms engaged in the process of saving, investing, and borrowing. The growth rates of a developing country's financial institutions and the contribution they make to the nation's savings performance are dependent on the government's macroeconomic policies. Appropriate policies are crucial in creating an environment of lender and investor confidence through the maintenance of political stability, steady economic growth with low inflation, and support for the private sector. Those who examine financial system problems and design alternative remedies should always keep in mind the ultimate needs of market participants.

Always Accompany Deregulation with Adequate Supervision

Too often, those in charge of deregulation have given short shrift to new requirements for supervision. The ultimate result is a wave of instability brought on by the excesses of freedom of action. Ironically, deregulation should often be accompanied by an increase in the staff level of the supervisory agency and almost certainly by increased training.

To the Extent Possible, Precede Liberalization with Improvements in Banking Management Capabilities

Bank officers who have pursued careers administering mandated policies are not prepared to cope with market forces such as price competitiveness, lending risk, portfolio management, etc.

Employ Phased-in Policy Reforms Where Possible to Allow Adjustment in Market Behavior and Avoid Excessive Swings

Dramatic shifts in such areas as portfolio requirements or interest rate ceilings can produce adverse consequences and often require policy reversals. A phased liberalization strategy can often permit gradual rather than radical shifts in behavior and financial flows.

Adopt Incentives for Prudent Financial Management

Very often eligibility for liberalized rules can be tied directly or indirectly to institutional performance. For example, banks that consistently meet prudential performance standards can become eligible for a relaxation in their portfolio holdings requirements. Such incentives reward sound banking practices and establish models for behavior.

Identify and Address Secondary Effects of and Constraints to Reform Measures

The elimination of interest rate ceilings does little for borrowers in the short run other than increase their cost of funds. Similarly, the abolition of credit allocation formulas may result in the complete withdrawal of lending to specific sectors. These and other side effects need to be addressed directly in the formulation of policy changes. In some cases compensatory measures will be required.

COMMON CONSTRAINTS TO LIBERALIZATION

One should not underestimate the difficulties of helping a developing country move toward greater reliance on market forces to determine the pricing and allocation of credit. Numerous problems confront any effort to implement financial liberalization. In many countries, market participants have established structures and procedures to cope with the symptoms of financial system repression. They may be loathe to adapt their behavior to meet the requirements created by market forces and competition.

For example, changes in interest rates profoundly affect the entire internal and external economy. The practices of relying on directed credits at subsidized rates and on preferential access to funds are deeply entrenched in many developing countries. They have long been the major tool for implementing government investment policies (or political or economic policies) and funneling resources to specific sectors or target groups. The privileged beneficiaries of these programs have a vested interest in their continuation and often form groups that vocally oppose reform programs.

Furthermore, government leaders in some countries have built up their constituencies by granting preferential access to cheap loans to their supporters. They will be reluctant to give up this source of patronage. Since the impact of financial policy change is felt throughout the society, reformers need to take concerted steps to develop constituencies to counter often powerful opposition blocs.

In addition, the introduction of market-oriented policies almost inevitably leads to a transitional process of "survival of the fittest." Disadvantaged groups might suffer in the near term from higher interest charges or a reduction in available credit. Accordingly, liberalization programs ideally should include initiatives to take into explicit consideration the needs of the poor or financially vulnerable groups that are adversely affected by reforms.

In the short run, liberalization also faces several important but less obvious constraints. If a government takes away or reduces the financial institution barriers to entry, it is assumed that new banks will form and begin to operate. The newly-formed private banks may draw away the depositors and borrowers who do not require subsidies and will repay their loans. The viability of government banks may be further impaired, and they may require larger fiscal support from the government if their operations are to continue.

As part of most reform efforts, developing country governments chronically running large budget deficits are encouraged to hold down interest rates to reduce the costs of servicing the national debt. For the same reason, these governments may also require local financial institutions to hold an excessive volume of low-yielding government securities to the detriment of banks' profitability and, in extreme cases, their viability. In trying to address these problems, the policy changes needed to start, sustain, and enlarge the scope for free market forces in the financial sector must be carefully planned and paced, politically feasible, and not too disruptive to the economy.

Other constraints may make liberalization and the formation of new banks difficult. One may be the limitation of specialized banking skills in the country. Another may be the lack of capital resources of existing or potential entrepreneurs with which to form a bank. A third constraint may be the lack of a sufficient market, as was the case for newly formed banks in New Zealand. The new banks lent to marginal customers, incurring losses as the riskier businesses failed to repay.

5 Understanding Privatization of Financial Institutions

Bank privatizations represent attempts by governments to invigorate and modernize their banking sectors. In turn, they hope to stimulate their economies through the acceleration of capital formation and the provision of efficient and expanded financial services. Successful privatizations are often accompanied by financial reforms because changing the ownership structures alone cannot solve all the problems of ineffective financial sectors. However, it can serve as a positive and important step in the right direction.

This chapter discusses various techniques to privatize banking institutions, touching on important issues such as profitability, concentration of wealth, and protection of minority investors and depositors, as well as various technical and financial requirements. The chapter also examines constraints on privatizing banking institutions and the differences between the divestiture of banking institutions and other government-owned nonfinancial entities.

EXPERIENCE WITH BANK PRIVATIZATION

Privatization within the financial sector has received much attention in recent years. Throughout the world, governments are privatizing financial institutions. In countries as diverse as Great Britain, France, Germany, the Philippines, Mexico, and Guinea, governments have made moves to return, or in some cases shift, banking functions to private hands. Many additional countries are seeking to learn from these nations' experiences.

In Europe, France, West Germany, Italy, and Spain have all privatized components of their financial sectors. France has probably been the most active, initiating nine full or partial privatizations. In each case, 10 percent of the shares were reserved for employees, and foreign investors were limited to 20 percent of the shares offered for sale. In many cases, the government privately sold between 30 and 50 percent of the shares to institutional investors as a security measure to guard against a take-over attempt. The French government has realized almost 58 billion French francs from these sales. It will be interesting to watch how the newly emerging democracies of Eastern Europe approach the issue of financial sector reform and privatization.

Chile, Mexico, and Jamaica have been the dominant financial sector privatizers in Latin America. Chile experienced two waves of privatizations: one in the 1970s, and a second in the 1980s. In the most recent privatization activity, the government has sold 12 banks, pension funds, and insurance companies to local and foreign private businesses, utilizing both private sales and public offerings. In a public offering that was oversubscribed by 170 percent, the government of Jamaica sold the National Commercial Bank to more than 30,000 Jamaicans, many of whom bought stock for the first time.

In May 1990, the Mexican government reinforced its support for privatizing its state-owned banks and voted to repeal the 1982 bank nationalization law. Shares in three banks—Multibanco de Mexico, Baupais, and Banamex—were sold to private investors in 1991 for over $3.5 billion. The immediate decrease in interest rates and the increase in investor interest in the stock market have already helped to energize the economy. Previous Mexican privatization efforts were meager in comparison. The government sold minority shares in three banks. In February 1987, 34 percent of Banco Nacional de Mexico (Banamex) was sold in a combination public offering and private sale, 12 percent to employees and 17 percent to selected bank customers. A 23 percent stake in the Banco de Comercio (Bancomer) was also sold. The following month, 34 percent of Banca Serfin was sold to staff and clients.

Among the more active "privatizers" in Asia are South Korea and Bangladesh. The Korean government has fully divested its shares in national commercial banks, and engaged in an additional privatization and two partial divestitures of regional or sectoral institutions. In 1982/83, the government placed its shares in commercial banks in private hands through private sales. Concerned about ownership control by a single large industrial group, the government plans to sell its holdings in the Korea Exchange Bank and part of its shares in the Industrial Bank of Korea and the Citizens National Bank.

The Bangladesh government returned the Pubali and Uttara Banks to private owners, and reduced its holdings in the Rupali Bank to 51 percent. (See Appendix for more details.)

Some African countries have also attempted to privatize some of their state-owned banks. Gambia and the Ivory Coast are perhaps the most prominent in this effort. In a first step toward the privatization through a public share offering of the Gambia Commercial and Development Bank, the bank was incorporated. In addition, the government sold its minority shareholdings of the National Standard Bank in a public offering. In a private sale, the government of the Ivory Coast returned the BNEC bank to private ownership.

GUIDELINES FOR FINANCIAL INSTITUTION PRIVATIZATION

Privatizations can be structured in many different ways, but the key to successful privatization is a custom-made approach that will meet the needs of the government, potential investors, and the public. Privatization approaches most appropriate to banking institutions include the sale of shares to the public, management, and employees; complete or partial divestiture to private buyers; commercialization or corporatization— these terms indicate strategies that require government enterprises to operate according to market principles similar to commercial enterprises; management contracts, sometimes in conjunction with stock flotation; and closure and liquidation. These approaches are discussed below.

Sale of Shares to the Public, Management and Employees

The sale of shares constitutes a transfer of ownership to an individual or a corporate entity. Along with the share goes the right to vote for the directors on the bank's board and on matters put before all the share-holders. The Jamaican case offers an excellent example of the divestiture of a bank through the sale of shares to the public and employees.

The sale of shares to the general public helps overcome the objection that government assets may be transferred to wealthier individuals in the country. In reality, a poor individual may not be able to afford even a single share of bank stock. This case would probably hold even if the par value of the shares were very low. However, any attempt to sell shares to persons beyond the economic elite will most likely be broadly supported. Chile enabled many lower income persons to become shareholders through its Popular Capitalism program. Share purchasers could make a five percent down payment and amortize the remainder over 15 years on a no-interest basis. As of late 1988, more than 100,000 individuals participated in this program by investing over $400 million in privatized businesses.

However, if the par value is set low in an attempt to attract many lower income buyers, it may mean that each shareholder's stake is so small that the subsequent earnings per share paid by the bank may mean little. Furthermore, these shareholders will be able to exert little control over management because of the dilution of control. Nor will they be able to ensure that prudent lending practices and administration are followed. Therefore, some institutional investment should be encouraged. Institutional investors will typically exert active control over bank boards to ensure that their investment is protected. The balance between institutional investor participation and that of the public is a key consideration in a stock flotation.

One of the major factors determining whether a stock flotation is possible is the past financial performance of the bank. Even if a bank has not been consistently profitable, perhaps due to its role in government economic programs, the bank may still be inherently viable. The bank could be profitable if it were not operating as a government bank pursing government-mandated goals or if it had prudent management. To achieve profitability, it may be necessary for the bank to be transformed into an autonomous corporation as an interim step. Corporatization is discussed further below.

The balance sheet of an institution may reflect the poor lending practices of past management, that is, there may be many uncollected or uncollectible loans. Approaches for dealing with such debts may include the transfer of these loans to the appropriate ministry (usually Finance or Treasury) or to the central bank for collection and write-offs.

Once the decision has been reached to divest all or part of the ownership of the bank through a stock flotation, eight steps need to be taken to complete the task.

The first step to be taken is auditing. In order to determine the exact financial position of the institution, it is necessary either to procure new financial reports or certify existing reports. These actions should be taken by independent auditors. Such reports should identify any financial contingencies that may affect the financial status of the institution in the future. Particular attention must also be paid to the value of the bank's loan portfolio. For example, all loans should be aged according to standard procedures.

If the audit reveals that the bank is not actually profitable, a financial specialist should prepare financial projections to identify steps to achieve profitability. It may be decided that the bank should be divested through a negotiated sale or perhaps corporatized. Or it may be better to negotiate the sale of the bank to another financial institution that can take appropriate steps to improve services and achieve profits. A stock flotation is possible if the audited statements of the bank indicate profitability.

The transfer of non-performing loans is the second step in this process. A government bank's portfolio is likely to have a certain number of uncollectible loans. These loans should be transferred to the appropriate government ministry or the central bank for collection or write-offs. These transfers will enhance the bank's balance sheet and improve its salability.

The third step is the design of protections for shareholders and secondary marketing facilities. Prior to the issue of stock in a thin capital market, it is indispensable that all shareholders have certain protections. First, a mechanism should be established for maintaining contact with all stockholders. An exact record of all shareholders, their names, addresses, and number of shares owned must be maintained by the bank. A voting mechanism must also be established and safeguarded for all holders of voting common stock. Next, shareholders should receive audited financial reports prepared by independent accountants on at least an annual basis. Finally, payment of dividends, if declared, should be paid to the shareholders. If a regulatory unit to guarantee that these protections are maintained is not in existence prior to the privatization, it should be established before the sale of shares proceeds.

Another important consideration for investors is the ability to re-sell their shares in case they need liquidity or decide they no longer want to hold the shares. In cases where a stock exchange exists, the registration of shares with the agency in charge of the stock exchange must be undertaken prior to their issuance. However, some countries have no exchange at all. In such cases a relatively informal exchange or "trading post" needs to be established to handle these transactions. Another possibility might be a buy-back arrangement whereby the company repurchases its own stock at a small discount from shareholders desiring liquidity.

The fourth step entails stock issuance, valuation, and pricing. It is generally necessary to issue new shares unless there has been a previous issue. This step involves the actual creation of stock certificates that specify its par value. Setting the par value is a function of the value of the bank, the buying power of the public, and the interest there may be in purchasing the issue.

The valuation of a financial institution varies substantially from that of an industry. However, the basic premise is the same. The value is based on how much the business can earn after taxes. The valuation of a bank may require two types of calculations to determine its worth—valuation of its components and valuation of the bank as a going concern. The components valuation approach involves loan portfolio valuation, core deposit valuation, and valuation of proprietary items, the name of the bank, etc.

For financial institutions, the audited balance sheet is a fairly good indicator of value. The loan portfolio is composed of financial instruments that state the terms and conditions of the loan. The loans must be aged to reflect collectibility. However, the balance sheet does not reflect potential future earnings. Therefore, a going concern valuation must be performed to avoid understating the bank's true value. Again, specialized valuation assistance can be obtained through an internationally-recognized valuation firm.

Once the value of the bank is established, then an appropriate share price can be set. Price setting requires a balance between the need to set prices low enough to ensure a strong demand for the shares and the need to avoid criticism that the government should have received more for the sale of the shares. Setting the price too high will lower demand. Once the par value is established it can be incorporated into the prospectus and the stock certificates can be printed.

A fifth step is preparation of a prospectus. A prospectus is a document providing full disclosure of all pertinent information about the financial institution. A prospectus should include a description of all assets and liabilities; profit and loss records for several years, based on an audit prepared by an independent auditing firm; a description of all outstanding issues of securities and terms; a list of all officers and directors, together with the salaries of the top officers; and identification of anyone presently holding 5 percent or more of the ownership.

A preliminary draft of the prospectus should be prepared before the price is set on the stock issue. In the United States, the preparation of a prospectus implies a level of fiduciary trust with legal liability in case false information is included in the document. Therefore, it is recommended that specialized assistance through an internationally-recognized investment banking or accounting firm be employed for the preparation of the prospectus.

Sixth is the share sale promotion and marketing. Once the prospectus is completed, it can be distributed to all persons interested in purchasing the shares. A problem found in many developing countries is that not many people are able to read or understand the technical contents of a prospectus. Furthermore, many people do not understand what it means to be a shareholder, what are the rights of shareholders, and when and why dividends are paid. A successful stock flotation in a developing nation requires a massive public education campaign.

Even in the United States, emphasis is placed on promoting the sale of shares to the public. This campaign should begin well in advance of the completion of the prospectus and the proposed issue date. It is advisable to utilize the services of a professional public relations firm. Radio, television, the press, and targeted presentations can arouse interest and educate the public.

The seventh step involves stock transfer to an executing agency. Some unit of government (an investment bank, or a consortium comprising investment banks, brokerages, etc.) should be made responsible for the sale of the shares. In case of a flotation of shares of a particularly strong bank, an investment bank might even underwrite the issue. However, in most cases these institutions only act as agents for the government, collecting a fixed fee or a commission on sales.

The eighth step involves the actual sale of the stock to the public. A mechanism should be established beforehand to allocate the shares in case the issue is over-subscribed. In the Jamaican case, a share allocation arrangement formula was established to ensure that smaller investors were given priority.

The public sale of shares as a means to privatize a financial institution is a complicated process. It involves a series of specialized services to ensure that each step is correctly executed and that the interests of both investors and the bank are protected. Privatization of banks in this manner has distinct advantages in spreading, not concentrating, wealth. This fact could pay excellent political dividends to the government, which could encourage the authorities to continue and expand privatization activities. Bank privatization through a sale of shares can also act to deepen domestic capital markets. However, the transaction will require time and considerable expense.

Complete or Partial Divestiture to Private For-Profit Institutions

Divestiture of a government-owned banking institution to a private sector group or financial institution tends to be an easier undertaking than the share sale process described above. The buyers interested in such a purchase might typically be a local business conglomerate controlled by family interests, a similar conglomerate that includes a financial institution desiring to expand its markets, or an international banking institution. One key to the success of such privatizations is that the buyer should bring bank management experience to the institution. Prospective buyers will be interested in the financial performance record of the bank, its financial potential, and the percentage of the operation that the government is willing to sell.

One disadvantage to this technique is that it can further concentrate wealth in the country, especially if sold to local, already wealthy business interests. Privatization could be seen as benefitting the rich at the expense of the poor. Furthermore, without proper supervision, the banks may skew their lending to meet their owners' needs, which may include bailing out companies in which the owners have a stake.

An international banking institution offering to buy a local bank could be a source of concern in countries where foreign investment is not viewed favorably. Nevertheless, international banks may be owed money by the government or individual institutions and may have the right under a debt-equity swap program to convert their debt to equity in a local business. An example of this is found in the Philippines, where government-acquired banks have been sold to international banks through debt-equity conversions.

Buyers will be especially interested if they are allowed to buy the majority share, or at least to exert effective control over the bank through the subordination of the government's voting rights. Such a bank should be able to install new management that can quickly take steps to improve its operations. This move could produce immediate economic benefits.

Another advantage in using this technique is that the bank to be privatized may be sold without demonstrating a record of profits. The buyer must be convinced, based on financial analysis, that the turned-around bank could be profitable and that the bank will not be subject to undue government interference that could jeopardize profits. A foreign buyer will also want guarantees that it can repatriate future profits. In order for the government to negotiate the private sale of banks, it must take several steps:

- Perform an independent audit certified by an independent, professional auditing firm.
- Perform a valuation of the bank.
- Assess what must be done concerning the bank's management and employees.

- Identify and address any legal obstacles.
- Prepare a "best available" information brochure for potential buyers.
- Provide ample time for potential buyers to make their own analyses to support their investment.

Using such an approach avoids the requirement of rehabilitating the bank prior to the sale. The government may be persuaded to transfer uncollectible and government agency loans to an appropriate ministry. However, steps to modernize the operation (computerizing the bank's record-keeping functions, etc.) should be left to the new buyers who can tailor changes to meet their own needs.

One of the most important steps for the government is to determine its obligations to the employees of the financial institution and to set forth the best means to fulfill those obligations. As government employees, most bank workers will have accrued pension and other benefits. These should be calculated and paid by the government upon sale of the operation. Furthermore, the new buyer may want to install its own management team but may want to retain the employees whose training and experience may be difficult to replace. One option is to include in the sales agreement a provision for retaining specified employees for a trial period of six to twelve months. If the employee is deemed suitable at the end of the period, he or she can be retained.

The "best available" information provides prospective buyers with all data on the banking operation for their consideration. Buyers will want to carefully examine the loan portfolio and will negotiate the purchase, in part, based on the aging of the bank's loans. Buyers will also want to examine legal agreements with creditors, such as loans provided by multilateral lending agencies, to determine the potential effects of the sale.

Commercialization/Corporatization

Commercialization or corporatization, the requirement that enterprises operate according to true commercial standards, is viewed as an interim step to divestiture. Corporatization is recommended when the financial institution is currently unprofitable but is viewed as having remediable deficiencies and strong potential profitability. The seven steps to be taken in establishing an autonomous corporation are as follows:

- A financial viability analysis that envisions the payment of amortizations, taxes, and dividends to the government is prepared.

- The government establishes a statutory corporation to which it will transfer the assets and the liabilities of the present government bank.
- Rehabilitation requirements are identified.
- A valuation of the assets of the bank is completed and a loan is made providing for repayment by the new statutory corporation.
- Arrangements are made for the transfer of personnel from the government payroll to the new corporation. Salary structures are examined to ensure compatibility with levels in similar private sector operations. A management contract with an international bank wherein a professional management team or advisors are placed in the bank to upgrade the banking procedures and systems and achieve profitability may be useful.
- The development of a new accounting system or adjustment of the present system is usually required.
- Arrangements for ongoing supervision and regulation of the corporation must be made.

These seven steps to restructure the bank may result in an improvement in its financial performance. However, the bank continues to be a government-owned bank even if it is attracting deposits and lending at market interest rates, paying taxes and dividends to the government, and amortizing the transfer price of the bank. Accordingly, there remains a possibility for the government to attempt to influence the lending practices of the bank.

In addition, the performance of the bank may be so dramatically improved that the government and the public no longer perceive the need to create a privately owned institution. In New Zealand in the mid-1980s, the Labour government lost credibility because it initially announced that it would limit its efforts to corporatizing banks, and subsequently determined that it should push for privatization. The lesson is that corporatization should only be viewed as a step toward ultimate privatization. Corporatization probably does not go far enough, and leaves open the opportunity for the government to return to previous non-economic practices. The ultimate step in an effective corporatization procedure is the issuance and sale of shares either on the local stock exchange or by the techniques described above.

Management Contracts

Contracting out the management of government-owned banks is another form of limited privatization. Management contracts may be especially useful in those instances when the government has no intention, at present, of divesting the state-owned bank. A management contract may demonstrate the financial performance of the institution under private sector incentives. In the case of corporatization, a management contract may be a necessary ingredient for achieving success with the newly structured institution. The selection of contractors and the structuring of the contract will have a strong influence over whether this arrangement achieves the desired results.

Potential contractors able to assemble sufficient bank management expertise may not exist domestically. Furthermore, contracts involving the management of competitor banks may have collusive results. Therefore, it may be necessary to establish a tendering process that includes expatriate bidders. Under all circumstances, a tendering process should be used. The elements of a management contract should include the following items:

- Management staffing, procedures, and costs for replacement of personnel
- Duration of contract with conditions for renewal
- Definition of duties, obligations, and rights
- Training of local staff
- Profit-sharing arrangements
- Clauses providing effective control of bank operations
- Reporting requirements, specifically to the board of the bank
- Clauses for resolving differences of opinions
- Conditions for termination

One of the most important clauses entitles the contractor to have a share of the profits. Sometimes these clauses are structured progressively; the more profits earned, the greater the remuneration received by the contractor. Such clauses may stimulate better financial performance.

Another important clause involves the effective control, without governmental interference, of operations. It is likely that the government may still want to impose its regime of credit allocation, the provision of subsidies, and similar uneconomic practices on the bank's operators. These regulations will not be changed unless the broader financial sector reforms discussed elsewhere in this book are instituted. Nevertheless, once the "rules of the games" are set for the bank's operations, it should be insulated from all but normal monetary and financial policies.

One advantage in utilizing a management contract is that it provides an opportunity for another banking group to become familiar with the banking markets in the country in the event of a divestiture of government-owned banks.

Closure and Liquidation

One of the most prevalent means to privatize state-owned enterprises (SOEs) to date has been informal privatization or closure. In these cases, the government has decided that continued operations mean further losses and requirements for often increased budgetary support. However, the government may not want to be perceived as "taking a step backward" by closing an operation. Moreover, it usually does not want to be seen as creating further unemployment.

The government in such situations may make the decision to provide no additional financial support. This step usually is sufficient to bring the SOE to insolvency within a short time period. The socialistically-oriented Guinean banks were allowed to decline to that point—in fact, it appears that those banks had become useless as deposit takers, and the only loans extended were to government agencies.

Such cases represent a good opportunity for the liberalization of entry requirements. New banks might be formed by local entrepreneurs or as a result of policies to encourage joint ventures between international banking operations and local entrepreneurs.

One advantage associated with liberalizing market entry policies is that the qualified personnel of the moribund government bank may be absorbed by the new banks. Thus, the tough political decisions required could be more palatable.

COMMON CONSTRAINTS TO PRIVATIZATION

The major constraints to privatization tend to lie in the implementation of the actual divestiture. These constraints crop up even after the political decision is made by the government to privatize certain government-owned companies.

Sales of publicly-owned banks are often resisted by the banks' managements. Accordingly, governments need to appoint independent bodies to carry out privatizations. The management of a government-owned bank typically would not find it advantageous to develop its own divestiture plan and, if approved, implement it. This case occurred with the Philippine National Bank (PNB). The Asset Privatization Trust asked PNB to develop its own divestiture plan, but the management resisted. To carry out privatization requires not only political decision-making on the part of the government but also the will to follow-through on its decisions. Independent, interventionist actions are usually required.

The government may want to retain the bank's management and employees if the bank is well-run and not subservient to private economic interests in the country, as in the divestiture of the Jamaican National Commercial Bank. However, careful planning involving fair treatment of employees to be dismissed, retired, or absorbed elsewhere must be undertaken if the management and employees are not to be retained. The representation of the employees by a labor union is a serious consideration and potential constraint. If the management and employees are to be replaced completely, the shortage of the specialized skills required in a banking institution in some countries may also act as a serious constraint.

An additional constraint may arise if the government is attempting to sell the bank to a group that owns a conglomerate of family or other concentrated economic interests. If seen as a step toward concentration of wealth, it may be resisted by the general public or specific interest groups. To avoid this problem, the Jamaican government limited the shareholding of any individual to 7.5 percent of the shares issued.

Another potential constraint may arise out of how the assets of the financial institution are valued. The valuation must satisfy both the government and its constituents that the government is not "giving away" or undervaluing the country's assets in the privatization transaction. Because the primary asset of any bank is its loan portfolio, there must be agreement as to the worth of the loan portfolio. The disposition of non-performing loans may also pose a constraint to privatization. Sometimes it will be impossible to divest the financial institution without ridding its balance sheet of uncollectible loans.

The lack of availability of financial data on the bank's operations may also serve as a constraint. Even in cases where audited financial data exist, the unreliability of financial statements and local accounting practices for valuing assets may serve as a constraint. Often the government feels it should receive the book value for SOEs privatized, and that position raises a severe constraint.

Certainly one of the bottlenecks to selling financial institutions through the issuance and flotation of shares has been perceived as the lack of well-developed capital markets, especially in smaller economies. The sale of the Commercial National Bank in Jamaica shows that need not be the case, even though that country's capital markets are very thin. The availability of informal sector funds for such investment, as demonstrated in the Bangladesh case, may be one of the positive effects registered as the privatization movement progresses.

Lack of knowledge about shareholding, even among middle-income individuals, may constitute another limitation to divestiture using flotation and share sales. A related constraint is that governments may not wish to relinquish ownership of profitable companies, despite the fact that profitability is fundamental to such share sales.

Certainly one of the major considerations for private buyers in a privatization is whether they can profit from their investment. Because many government-owned banks have been used as an instrument of government socioeconomic policies, there may have been little concern for the financial performance of the bank. A prudent lending program may not have been the practice, and lending may have been directed to infeasible or uneconomic activities. As a result, collections may have been low, yielding poor financial results. Furthermore, the expectations of borrowers regarding loan repayment may be such that collections may be difficult during the early years after privatization.

As discussed, because the government's financial and monetary policies directly affect a bank's profitability, those policies may create a major constraint to privatization. For example, if the central bank requires reserves be held in below-market yielding government securities or the interest rate regime does not allow an adequate spread given the level of risk, it may be difficult to sell the bank until those policies are changed. For this reason, it has been stressed elsewhere in this book that financial reform and deregulation (not jeopardizing prudent supervision and oversight) are recommended as a desirable complementary activity.

The ability to make a profit also depends on whether there is sufficient market potential for an aggressive but prudent lender. Prospective buyers will want to carefully study the bank's market potential if the bank to be privatized has primarily focused its lending on borrowings by the government or government-related activities.

If the financial performance of the bank has been poor, the government may not want to divest it outright; the sale could yield considerably more if the bank were rehabilitated. This was the case of three banks under consideration for privatization in New Zealand. Expenditures running into the millions of dollars were made by the government to upgrade and computerize information systems and to generally modernize the bank's operations. Such expenditures may be appropriate if a broad stock flotation is envisioned; however, extensive rehabilitation may be inappropriate if the bank is to be sold to another financial institution. In the latter instance, the buyer could best undertake the required rehabilitative steps according to its own strategy and requirements.

In some countries where divestitures to local buyers is acceptable, sales to foreign investors or financial institutions may create a wave of resistance. Certainly the prospect of foreign ownership can create a political constraint. In the Philippines, where prospects of foreign investment dominating sectors worries the local business community, several banks have been privatized using debt-equity swaps. In such cases, international banks that were owed money by individual parties or the Philippine government have converted these uncollectible loans to equity in government-owned banks. The government has had to balance its need to reduce external debt with its concern about foreign investment. Debt-equity swap programs may actually increase the antagonism toward foreign investors in some developing countries.

In some countries, though, it may be necessary to encourage some foreign investment to overcome the constraints of limited capital or bank management experience and capability. These arrangements are often made more palatable when administered in the form of a joint venture with the government or local investors. The Guinea government entering into joint ventures with three French banks offers an excellent example of how one country overcame such constraints in order to strengthen and expand nearly defunct domestic banking services in a short period of time.

In summary, a series of constraints affects the prospects for both privatization and liberalization in many developing countries. Privatization and liberalization must be viewed as primarily political processes, and each privatization program needs to be tailored to overcome its particular constraints.

6 Developing a Framework for Financial Reform and Privatization

Countries that embark on a course of financial reform and privatization are likely to experience a number of important benefits. The economic performance of developing countries can be materially and in some cases dramatically strengthened as a direct consequence of improvements in the efficiency and stability of their financial systems. The central thesis of this book is that such improvements can be achieved through two sets of initiatives—privatization and financial policy reform. *Privatization* allows for financial decision-making to be placed in private hands, thereby establishing strong efficiency and profit motives as the driving forces behind financial intermediation. *Policy reform* serves as a means to increase the role of market forces in the determination of interest rates, the allocation of credit, and the overall scale of financial intermediation. In addition, policy reforms can work to strengthen the financial soundness of the sector, encourage more efficient business practices, and provide savers and investors with a wider breadth of financial services and instruments.

Privatization and policy reform should be viewed as complementary strategies, not as substitutes (see Figure 6.1). The attainment of a policy climate that is conducive to market forces is a requisite for successful privatization since the introduction of private management and ownership into a hostile, repressed financial environment will almost invariably lead to disappointing results. Similarly, the creation of an appropriate policy framework in a system dominated by government owned and operated institutions achieves less than if privatization were also undertaken.

Overall liberalization creates incentives for all market participants, whereas privatization is targeted at individual institutional actors. Simi-

Figure 6.1
Methods for Improving Financial Sector Performance: Macroeconomic and Financial Sector Reform and Privatization

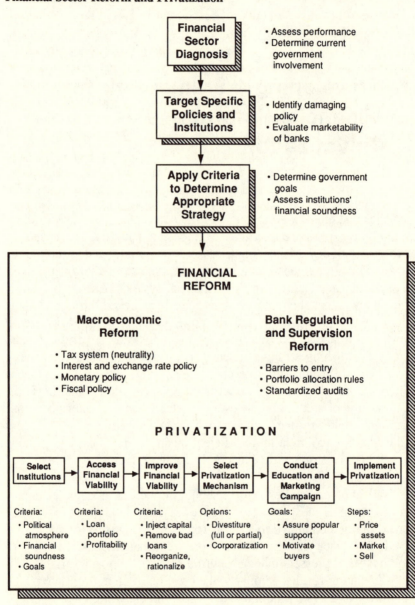

larly, policy reform can over time achieve some of the goals of privatization through the establishment and gradual expansion of new, private sector institutions. However, the implementation of appropriate financial policies is far more complex and difficult than the discreet sale of SOEs.

The design and execution of reform packages often requires strong political will, extensive understanding of interrelationships within the system, and a delicate sense of timing. The absence of any of these attributes can lead to disappointing or counterproductive results. Nevertheless, the achievement of truly effective financial market reform in many developing countries requires the simultaneous pursuit of both policy change and privatization.

The benefits of financial liberalization and privatization are significant. Nations that undertake these measures set the foundation for healthy financial market development by encouraging all market participants, both on the saving and on the borrowing side of the equation, to participate in bank intermediation (see Table 6.1).

When a country has successfully reduced inflation, implemented appropriate interest and exchange rate policies, and encouraged the establishment of a competitive, private banking sector, savers will no longer be encouraged to speculate in real estate and other real assets or to hold foreign currencies and assets overseas. Instead, savings will be directed toward productive domestic investment. With more attractive returns and a greater breadth of available services, the rate of savings should also increase. Capital that previously was invested in government securities as required by law will be available to fund private businesses.

Both reform and privatization can pave the way for further innovation and the introduction of new savings instruments with attractive returns, which are likely to encourage additional saving. Macroeconomic reform will have this effect by means of stabilizing inflation and the value of the currency. It thereby allows savers to return to paper instruments denominated in local money. Privatization will encourage this result because the strengthened profit motive will push banks to innovate in order to attract new resources. Higher domestic savings rates will reduce dependence on expensive foreign capital and provide additional funds for growth.

Adopting the measures recommended in this book will also result in an improved allocation of scarce capital. Currently, large quantities of capital in developing countries—over half of all capital available in some nations—are invested by law in low-yielding government securities or are channeled to unproductive, government-selected projects, often with little hope for repayment in the short term. Once the government scales

Table 6.1
Benefits of Bank Privatization, Macroeconomic Reform, and Regulatory Reform

Bank Function	Privatization Will Improve Bank Performance	Macroeconomic Reform Will Improve Bank Performance	Regulatory Reform Will Improve Bank Performance	Economic and Societal Benefits of Improved Performance
Operate Efficiently	✓			Lower intermediation costs, increase savings and investment
Mobilize Resources	✓	✓	✓	Increase capital formation
Develop Financial Products	✓		✓	Reduce capital flight
Allocate Credit Among Alternate Investments	✓	✓	✓	Increase efficiency of investments, speed economic development
Collect Loans	✓		✓	Allocate costs fairly, reduce strain on government budgets
Recruit and Supervise Personnel	✓			Lower intermediation costs, create higher quality work force
Maintain Fiduciary Relationships	✓		✓	Increase savings, reduce capital flight
Minimize Corruption in Banking Sector			✓	Increase bank confidence, increase pool of investment funds

back its expenditures and reduces the scope of directed credit, and once banks are allowed to pursue profitable lending opportunities, larger amounts of capital will flow toward private investments that are productive and generate a sufficient cash flow to ensure loan repayment.

Reform and privatization will not only encourage more intermediation but also engender greater efficiency in intermediation. Lower administrative costs, reduced reserves for bad loans, and diminished mandatory purchases of low-yielding government securities will all work to diminish the wedge between interest paid to savers and interest charged to borrowers. As the spread becomes smaller, interest rates can rise for savers and fall for borrowers, thus further encouraging saving and investing.

The remainder of this chapter presents a framework for pursuing an economic growth strategy based on both financial reform and privatization. As is the case with other initiatives, the exact and appropriate course of action depends on a number of variables, including economic, institutional, political, and social factors, many of which are intricately interwoven.

A checklist for financial reform and privatization to assist governments designing such policies and programs is presented in Figure 6.2. Although no such list could anticipate every issue that may arise in a given situation, this checklist attempts to guide program designers from an initial diagnosis of the financial markets, through the selection of policy and program options, to their final implementation.

DIAGNOSE THE CURRENT FINANCIAL SECTOR

The first stage toward financial reform and privatization is analysis to determine the problems facing the sector and their causes. Initial data gathering should focus on the types of financial institutions and services provided locally, the extent of usage of the formal financial system by both savers and borrowers, and the size of the informal sector. Few services, low usage, and a large informal financial sector all point to a severely constrained or "repressed" banking system.

An "audit" of government policies toward the financial sector is a first step in determining the constraints on the sector. The review of policies should closely examine the extent of interest rate ceilings and controls, the percentage of total credit that is directed by the government toward specified sectors, the existence of excessive reserve requirements, and the effect of exchange rate policies on local savings and investment.

Figure 6.2
Checklist for Financial Reform and Privatization

CHECKLIST ITEMS

☐ *Diagnose Financial Sector*

  ☐ **Assess sector's range and efficiency of financial intermediation services**

    ☐ Types of services provided.

    ☐ Assess usage (by both savers and investors) of formal financial channels, and estimate real growth rates.

    ☐ Assess magnitude of informal sector.

  ☐ **Conduct audit of government policies toward the financial sector. Focus analysis on:**

    ☐ Existence of interest rate ceilings and controls.

    ☐ Degree of directed credit and existence of excessive reserve requirements.

    ☐ Effect of exchange rate policies on local savings and investment.

  ☐ **Estimate degree of competition in financial markets**

    ☐ Collect data on number of institutions and market shares.

    ☐ Identify government policies that limit types of institutions and range of services.

    ☐ Identify government-owned institutions (often not as straightforward as it may appear).

☐ *Target Specific Policies and Institutions*

  ☐ **Determine government goals. Different goals will point toward very different policy and program directions.**

  ☐ **Begin policy dialogue on government policies that are most damaging to financial sector performance.**

  ☐ **Assess political will for privatization.**

  ☐ **Evaluate saleability of banks, market conditions, and soundness of overall economy.**

☐ *Undertake Financial Reforms*

  ☐ **Design and implement any macroeconomic reforms needed. In particular, work toward the following policies:**

    ☐ Positive real interest rate, and low inflation.

    ☐ Credit allocation based on risk and return.

    ☐ Competitive exchange rates.

    ☐ Budget deficits that do not crowd out private investment and do not fuel inflation through the printing of money.

76

Figure 6.2 (continued)

☐ Craft and put in place regulatory and supervisory changes. Strive to achieve the following:

    ☐ Low barriers to entry in banking and other financial services (but adequate capital requirements to ensure stability). Allow private banks to operate. Consider allowing some role for foreign banks.

    ☐ Audited bank statements, and audited financial records for bank clients.

    ☐ Establish and enforce prudential capital adequacy ratios.

    ☐ Self-regulation to the extent possible. Reward compliance with regulations with additional flexibility in investing assets.

    ☐ Supervisory personnel in adequate numbers and with enough qualifications to effectively oversee bank operations and detect problems early .

☐ *Review privatization options, and move toward private sector ownership of financial institutions.*

    ☐ Select institution to privatize, based on government goals, political will, and readiness of institution for private sale.

    ☐ Assess financial viability. Expert technical assistance may be needed.

    ☐ Improve financial viability. Determine the extent to which banks must be improved via removal of nonperforming loans, reorganization, implementation of management information system, etc., prior to sale and what tasks can be left for the buyer. Evaluate alternatives for removing non-performing loans from bank portfolio. Inject new capital. Reorganize and rationalize operations.

    ☐ Select privatization mechanism depending on institution to be sold and market characteristics. Public offerings can work even in emerging stock markets. Private offerings may be faster but more vulnerable to political opposition. Corporatization (implementing management systems and procedures such as those used in private business) can be a useful first step, but move to privatize before political will dissipates.

    ☐ Conduct educational and marketing campaign regardless of privatization option chosen, but especially prior to a public offering. Political opposition is often the primary obstacle to privatization. Campaign will work to minimize opposition, and maximize participation in sale.

    ☐ Implement privatization option. Timing is critical, especially for a public offering.

The audit should also highlight the structure of the current financial system, determining the degree of competition in financial markets and the extent of government ownership. It should estimate the number of institutions in important niches (commercial banks, savings banks, credit unions) and their respective market shares. It should also identify government-owned institutions, a task often complicated by the fact that many different local, regional, and national agencies will own stakes in a single institution.

TARGET SPECIFIC POLICIES AND INSTITUTIONS

Whether a government places primary emphasis on financial reform or privatization depends on its goals. A country seeking to encourage savings and productive investment and stabilize its currency should focus on financial reform. In contrast, a nation concerned about large government subsidies to banks, inefficient bank administration, and a lack of competition among banks should concentrate its efforts on transferring banks to private ownership. However, without first creating a macroeconomic and regulatory environment that is conducive to financial sector development, privatization in and of itself will not achieve the desired results. The policy audit will indicate whether a government needs to focus on its economic and regulatory policies or whether positive policies are already in place.

If it appears that enough of the policy framework is in place to allow privatization to generate some benefits, the next step is to assess whether the political will exists to initiate and follow through on a privatization plan. Political opposition is the most important obstacle to privatization and a common reason for a slow-down or abandonment of privatization plans. For this reason, policy planners should closely monitor prevailing views and the political power of groups such as organized labor, the government bureaucracy in charge of the state-run institutions, and opposition political parties. If opposition is too intense, planners should select a less visible privatization option such as corporatization, an increase in private capital, or a joint venture. Any successful privatization effort must include a campaign strategy to minimize opposition, either through building constituencies of proponents of the program or by co-opting potential opponents. A strong communication component is vital to obtain popular, broad-based support.

Policymakers should also assess market conditions, including the readiness of various institutions for sale, the availability of local capital, and the general health of the economy. Many institutions must be groomed prior to a sale. Likewise, most developing countries will need an aggressive marketing campaign, and perhaps even subsidized financing terms, in order to absorb a large privatization.

APPLY CRITERIA TO DETERMINE APPROPRIATE STRATEGY

Table 6.2 summarizes criteria for determining an appropriate strategy. These criteria fall into several categories: macroeconomic climate, government goals, degree of financial market competition, political will, institutions' financial soundness, market conditions, and soundness of the economy. Each of these issues is discussed below.

Macroeconomic Climate for Financial Sector Development

Ownership of individual institutions is less important until the macroeconomic forces on savings, intermediation, and investment behavior are positive and not negative. Financial reform should precede or accompany privatization in nearly all cases.

As the preceding sections demonstrated, high and variable inflation, negative real interest rates, and overvalued exchange rates are anathema to the development of financial markets. Other policies common in developing countries also hinder growth in capital markets. These include a weak or unenforced contract law (thereby allowing borrowers who fail to repay their obligation to evade retribution) and weak bank regulation and supervision. Little else can be done to improve the functioning of financial markets until these obstacles are removed.

Thus, "stand-alone privatization" is unlikely to have the desired effect of improving the efficiency and effectiveness of financial markets. Changing the incentives for bank management and staff by making them more responsive to profit-making opportunities will not improve performance if the entire financial sector remains protected from competitive forces in the form of market-determined interest rates and exchange rates. Privatization can only work within a climate of suitable economic policies and legal/regulatory structures.

Government Goals

The appropriateness of financial reform versus privatization is also largely a function of a government's goals. Financial reform is the most

Table 6.2
Criteria for Selecting Financial Reform or Privatization

	Criteria	Policy and Program Response
1.	Macroeconomic climate for financial sector development	Until interest rates, exchange rate policy, and directed credit programs encourage savings and allocate loans appropriately, focus on improving the policy environment.
2.	Government goals	Certain goals are best accomplished through financial sector reform, including the provision of a business climate conducive to growth, promotion of exports and savings, and economic stabilization. Other goals, such as reducing strain on the government budget and boosting efficiency of financial markets are met through privatization of banks.
3.	Competitiveness of local financial markets	If government banks operate under more restrictive rules than private banks, remove restrictions before privatizing. To the extent that competition encourages government-owned banks to mimic private banks, privatization becomes less important than financial reform.
4.	Political will	In the face of opposition, generate financial sector efficiency through financial sector reform, which usually is not the focus of intense labor union and public opposition.
5.	Financial soundness of banks	The time is right for privatization only if the banks being sold are attractive to private buyers. Governments may need to improve balance sheets by dealing with nonperforming loans.
6.	Market conditions	The lack of a functioning stock market need not stymie privatization. Many options exist, including allowing the emergence of new private banks and joint ventures with foreign capital and management expertise.
7.	Soundness of economy	If possible, postpone public offerings and private sales until local economy is healthy enough to generate interest in the sale and a fair price.

appropriate path to the extent that the government's interests lie in providing a framework conducive to business, in promoting exports, in rewarding saving behavior, and in stabilizing the national currency. In contrast, privatization is the best alternative if the government's objective is to reduce the drain of unprofitable SOEs on the national budget, increase competition in financial markets, boost efficiency of financial markets, and distribute ownership of government-owned assets among the populace.

Competitiveness of Local Financial Markets

If government-owned institutions are operating in local financial markets in direct competition with private banks, and under the same operating rules (especially rules regarding interest rates and directed credit), then privatization becomes less necessary. The combination of an appropriate macroeconomic and regulatory framework for financial markets and competitive pressures will bring about many of the benefits of direct private ownership. As long as the government is somewhat vigilant about requiring adequate financial performance from its banks, pressure from private institutions will encourage the public banks to "keep up," and offer attractive instruments and good service. If private banks coexist with government-owned banks, then governments should probably focus their efforts on improving the economic and regulatory framework for all financial institutions, regardless of ownership, and assign secondary importance to the transfer of the SOEs to the private sector.

Political Will

Privatization is ultimately a political decision, even though it is often based at least partially on economic criteria and goals. Inasmuch as it is the transfer of ownership from the public to a group of private individuals, privatization most directly affects three groups of individuals: the previous owners (the general public), the employees, and the new owners (the private individuals). The general public is usually concerned about the price at which "their" good is sold; the employees are worried about job security. These two issues are often the major obstacles to privatization. Both should be carefully considered when selecting a privatization method.

The sale price of an SOE often becomes politicized when it has a market value below book value because of mismanagement and/or excessive liabilities. If the general public views a low sale price to a group of private investors as a "gift to the rich," then opposition to the sale may result. Similarly, organized labor's concerns about layoffs following a transfer to private ownership can sometimes effectively block a sale.

The strength of potential opposition and the popularity of the government should both be assessed prior to choosing a privatization method. Public opinion should be continually monitored as the privatization program proceeds. Governments can use a variety of techniques to minimize public opposition to a sale. To the extent that macroeconomic and regulatory reform will bring about the needed changes in bank behavior, such reforms can typically be implemented without generating the intense political opposition that privatization tends to generate. Another technique to diffuse public wariness is to undertake privatization in two steps, with the first step being an inflow of new private equity into a government-owned bank, perhaps through a joint venture. The transfer of government shares would follow later. In addition, the "packaging" of the privatization is extremely important. A publicity campaign can point out the benefits of the sale, such as reduced public spending and better service. Such campaigns have proven very successful in Jamaica. When the public is antagonistic to privatization, the word "privatization" should be avoided, and phrases such as "opening up to private capital," "popular capitalism," or "restructuring" should be used in its place.

Labor opposition must also be included in the decision to privatize. Partial employee buyouts, at subsidized terms, are one way to grant some of the benefits of the sale to the workers and thus encourage support for the sale. Labor often requires some guarantee of job security, which can be paid for either by the new owner or, if that is not feasible, by the government.

Financial Soundness of Institutions

Government-owned banks often need cosmetic (and even structural) surgery on their balance sheets before they are attractive to private capital. Governments cannot expect to sell a highly indebted SOE in a standard public offering. At the same time, extensive restructuring, implementing management information systems, and writing off bad loans can be extremely expensive and time consuming.

Whether the government or the new owner takes the write-offs for bad loans depends on each side's assessment of the bank's worth as well as on each side's relative negotiating strength. Governments attempting to place SOEs in thin markets are at a disadvantage compared to those with many potential buyers. Governments may be forced to accept a lower price or a less attractive transfer arrangement than would have emerged from competitive bidding. As in Chile, governments may need to improve the financial soundness of institutions prior to privatization. If possible, given the financial position of the SOE and degree of competition among potential buyers, the government should craft a mechanism that shares the responsibility and expense for past bad loan decisions between the new owners, who will benefit from future profits, and the past owners (the government), who were at least partially responsible for the decisions made.

Market Conditions

Weak or nonexistent capital markets are often touted as a serious constraint on privatization. However, the analysis of bank privatizations in this book indicates that the constraint is not as severe as is commonly thought. Many countries with only emergent capital markets, such as Jamaica, were able to utilize their stock markets to privatize SOEs. The thinner the stock market, the more important an educational and promotional campaign becomes, and the greater the need to subsidize stock purchases by the general public.

Countries that lack stock markets must turn to alternative privatization methods. But such techniques are numerous, and therefore the lack of a functioning stock market does not mean that privatization is impossible. Nations such as Guinea and Bangladesh utilized options that allowed the emergence of new, private banks to compete with government banks and attracted foreign capital and management to joint ventures with government banks. Both techniques proved successful.

Soundness of the Economy

Commitment to privatization, in any form, must be accompanied by the adoption of a policy environment that allows for competition and the operation of market forces in the sector in which the enterprise exists or an activity is performed. Economic activity must be open to competitive market forces (with no laws, regulations, or subsidies that would deter competition with what was the state-owned enterprise). Little will be gained from privatization if privatized enterprises are protected from market forces.

UNDERTAKE FINANCIAL REFORMS

Armed with a list of needed policy adjustments, policymakers should begin to work for change. The priority assigned to each policy change will vary depending on local conditions. In general, primary policy goals will be positive real interest rates, credit allocation based on risk and return rather than on pre-selected priorities, and competitive exchange rates. Other critical objectives include low inflation, a tax system that is neutral between debt and equity finance, and budget deficits that do not significantly crowd out private investment and are not financed through excessive, inflationary printing of money.

It is likely that adjustments in bank regulation and supervision will be needed in addition to the macroeconomic changes. Required reforms may include a reduction in barriers to entry for local private or foreign banks, a requirement that bank clients (and the banks themselves) furnish audited financial statements, and the establishment and enforcement of prudent capital adequacy ratios. Policymakers should support the creation of banking associations that can police certain aspects of member behavior, thus removing government interference while still ensuring banking safety. In order to monitor bank performance effectively in the face of increased freedom resulting from reforms, it may be necessary to increase staff levels and training for bank overseers.

SELECT AND IMPLEMENT PRIVATIZATION OPTIONS

If the political situation will allow privatization (and if the macroeconomic and regulatory reforms have taken place that will allow privatization to produce benefits), then the government should assess the readiness of both the financial institution and the market for the sale. This determination will be in part technical, based on expert appraisal of the bank's current value and future prospects, and in part political, based on an assessment of who is likely to buy the bank and an understanding of how the sale will be perceived.

Certain banks will need cosmetic surgery on the balance sheets or even more fundamental rehabilitation prior to being offered for sale. A variety of options exist, including removing non-performing loans from the bank's books, injecting new capital, and reorganizing and rationalizing operations, such as implementing a computerized management information system. The government should assess what measures need to be taken to make the bank attractive to private capital, keeping in mind that there is a trade-off between price and bank rehabilitation. The less the government does to improve the bank balance sheet, such as removing non-performing loans, the lower the selling price is likely to be. A government anxious to implement a rapid sale can choose not to improve the bank's balance sheet, but it will receive a lower selling price. In some cases it may be necessary for the government to pay an institution to take over the public bank, as is the case for many U.S. savings and loan institutions currently under supervisory control. In some situations, the most practical option may be to close the public bank.

The government should then select an appropriate privatization methodology, choosing from a variety of options including public share offerings, private sales, disbanding government banks and authorizing new private institutions, reorganizations, and/or employee buyouts. Governments facing great political opposition may want to consider maintaining public ownership while also creating more independent institutions that are self-financing and act more like private banks. This process is sometimes referred to as corporatization or commercialization. It is one way to improve bank performance without much publicity or fanfare. Commercialization can include reducing controls, portfolio requirements and subsidies for government banks, entering into private management contracts, encouraging competition with private institutions, and increasing the autonomy granted to existing bank management. Commercialization is a useful first step toward readying an institution for eventual sale.

Lack of a functioning stock market is no reason to avoid privatization. While undeveloped capital markets necessarily limit the options available to the government and make a public offering difficult or perhaps impossible, there nonetheless exist a number of options that do not require a stock market, such as a private sale or corporatization.

Regardless of the privatization mechanism chosen, an aggressive educational and marketing campaign is almost always needed. A promotional effort is a powerful means to advertise the benefits of privatization (or steps leading to eventual privatization) and defuse potential opposition. Such a campaign is essential to a large public offering in a country unaccustomed to offerings. Supported by strong media activity, large public offerings have been successful in countries without well-developed stock markets, such as Jamaica.

The last step is the implementation of the privatization. Timing is critical at this point. A public offering that coincides with a sudden drop in stock prices will greatly reduce government revenues from the sale. It may also diminish public confidence in the long-run profitability of the shares. To the extent possible, governments should schedule both private and public share offerings to take advantage of rising market prices and a healthy economic forecast.

The recommendations made above do not apply to every situation. However, they are based on a careful scrutiny of many cases of financial reform and privatization worldwide. Thus they should be useful in assisting governments to design policies and programs that promote the healthy development of financial markets.

SHORT-TERM COSTS INCURRED

As with all policies and programs, reform and privatization are likely to bring about some undesirable effects in the short term. In particular, interest rates are likely to rise for both savers and borrowers, raising banks' costs for acquiring funds and raising the cost to those businesses that previously had access to subsidized funds. Financial reforms that raise rates for savers may diminish bank profitability. Of course, banks will attempt to pass along these higher costs to their borrowing clients. Those clients used to borrowing at subsidized rates, such as managers of "politically connected" projects or firms in industries that the government encouraged, will be hard-pressed to pay the new higher rates, especially if their projects do not generate a sufficient return. These clients are likely to be vociferous opponents to financial reform and privatization. Their political connections should be considered prior to embarking on a strategy to improve financial markets. Higher interest rates could dampen investment in the short run. However, since higher interest rates are the result of an improved capital allocation process, the efficiency gains from better investment can counteract the potential reduction in investment.

Another negative repercussion of privatization and financial reform may be increased fraud. With some exceptions, direct government ownership and regulation (as opposed to supervision) seem more effective at controlling corruption. Strong measures should be taken to guard against increased fraud, including collusion, in the wake of reform and privatization. Not only is the fraud itself undesired but also publicity regarding such occurrences would jeopardize any further reform and privatization attempts. For example, knowledgeable observers in Mexico point to diminished bank corruption under government ownership.

A third common difficulty that arises in conjunction with financial reform and privatization is that generally weak bank managements, accustomed to operating within severely restricted parameters, find themselves free to make a wide variety of decisions they have never before faced. As occurred in Chile, a new-found freedom of action can result in poor decisions as bank managements climb the learning curve toward balancing portfolios, selecting high quality loan candidates, and operating effectively in a competitive environment. Because of this tendency, it is important to strengthen bank management skills when new policies are adopted.

Bank supervision should also be strengthened at or prior to financial market liberalization. Ironically, the size and quality of bank supervision staffs should grow at the same time many bank decisions are handed back to the banks. By decreasing direct control but increasing supervision, governments will move toward building a foundation for financial sector growth, monitoring the sector, and identifying problem areas. The private banks will, however, have the opportunity to innovate, expand, and develop.

Excessive concentration of bank ownership and troublesome business/bank linkages are a final negative effect that might result more from privatization than from financial reform. As was painfully illustrated in the Chilean privatization of the early 1970s, extensive bank ownership by large corporate groups can lead to unsound lending decisions and bank failure. The private sale of banks to large businesses can also engender public resentment if it is perceived as the sale of public assets to the wealthy, especially if the price is viewed as too low. These concerns should be carefully considered as privatization is planned, and attempts should be made to ensure widespread public ownership.

Concerns have been raised that the widespread ownership resulting from an aggressively marketed public offering is perhaps too thinly diffused, leaving control in the hands of the same bank management that operated the institution prior to the sale. For this reason, it is useful to approach a local or foreign institutional investor, such as an insurance company, pension fund, or another financial institution, to buy a significant but not controlling share in the bank to be privatized. This "lead owner" will have a strong stake in the bank's performance as well as the technical knowledge to assess bank decisions, oversee bank operations, and challenge the existing management if needed.

In spite of these possible negative repercussions, financial reform and privatization remain as key steps toward broad-based economic development. Care should be taken to minimize downside risks and to prepare the public to accept minor short-term adjustments. Without financial liberalization and privatization to provide businesses with access to credit, prospects for medium-term and long-term economic growth will remain poor.

7 Conclusion

Effective capital markets are indispensible to the pursuit of sustained, broad-based economic growth. Financial systems are dynamic. They continually change to meet evolving patterns of savings, fiscal conditions, institutional arrangements, and availability of and demand for funds.

In the broadest sense, an efficient, well-developed financial system offers many benefits to a country and its citizenry. These include:

- Making a country's financial system and its political and economic environment more stable.

- Helping promote growth and employment by expanding the range of financial instruments, offering investors different combinations of risk and reward, which, in turn, help raise the total volume of domestic savings and investment.

- Helping to promote democratic institutions and greater public participation in economic growth by opening up opportunities for more people to be involved in the financial system.

- Facilitating access to international capital as foreign investors are encouraged by efficient financial markets because they generally prefer to invest in countries where their funds are complementing, rather than replacing domestic savings.

The excessive presence of LDC governments in their financial systems, either through direct participation in the form of the state-owned financial institutions or through excessive controls on private financial activity, has inhibited LDC financial sector development. Government interference has restricted capital formation, reduced the financial system's flexibility (due to the smaller amount of funds available for lending and investing), and increased the costs of financial intermediation.

In this book, we have advocated a financial systems development strategy based on financial policy reform and privatization. Recognition is growing of the importance of economic growth strategies that combine financial sector reform and privatization. Among the issues requiring attention in the development of a combined strategy are the relationship between a supportive policy environment and a successful reform/privatization strategy; the importance of competition and the relaxation of entry barriers to a successful policy reform and deregulation effort; and the importance of broadening the ownership base in a privatization program.

Privatization is a phenomenon of only the past several years. However, its momentum is building. There is a similar growing appreciation of the importance of financial sector policy reform. The benefits of combining the privatization of state-owned financial institutions and the liberalization of LDC financial systems are enormous and spread beyond the financial system itself. Many developed and newly industrialized countries have pursued complementary reform/privatization strategies in the financial sector. Australia, Brazil, Chile, France, Italy, Mexico, New Zealand, and South Korea have all privatized banks and reduced restrictions on financial activity.

The movement toward more open and pluralistic societies and economies in Eastern Europe and Latin America offer important opportunities to take advantage of the growing recognition of financial reform/privatization strategies as effective mechanisms for economic growth. It is hoped that the issues raised and guidelines presented in this book will help government officials, private sector leaders, and donor agency professionals bring unsophisticated financial systems into a market-based framework that allows their citizenry to participate in their financial systems and their economies.

Appendix: Case Studies

Bangladesh:
Divestiture and Reduced Barriers to Entry: A Dual Track Privatization Policy

SUMMARY

Since 1982 when Bangladesh announced a general economic liberalization to encourage a greater role for the private sector, the private sector has gained control of a significant portion of the country's banking assets. In 1981, no local private banks existed; six state-owned commercial banks controlled about 93 percent of banking assets. By 1988, nine local private banks were in operation and about 45 percent of bank lending was conducted by private or autonomous institutions. However, like many of Bangladesh's reform efforts, the accomplishments had not met original goals. While the structure of ownership of banking assets changed dramatically, the financial sector was still dominated by state-owned or controlled banks that continued to base decisions as much on political criteria as on economic ones. Moreover, fundamental financial sector policy reform had not yet been implemented. Interest rates remained controlled and banks retained non-performing loans on their books at full value. A recent World Bank financial sector loan included conditionality to change these matters, but only time can tell if the measures will be implemented as designed.

Increasing the role of the private sector was accomplished with a dual track privatization policy. It included both full and partial divestiture of state-owned institutions and more importantly, a reduction in the barriers to entry for private institutions. The two smallest state-owned banks were fully divested through public offerings in 1984-1985, and 20 percent of a third state-owned bank was sold in 1988. Lowered barriers to entry led to the establishment of six new private local banks in 1982-1983. A seventh bank, an Islamic bank, was established in 1987.

These private banks are the most dynamic and thriving part of the banking sector and have contributed significantly to a large increase and deepening of Bangladesh's financial sector. Much of the private sector's success is, however, due to continued mismanagement and forced unprofitable lending within the remaining state-owned banks, which still dominate banking. If these state-owned institutions were more efficient and were not forced to operate under different rules than the private banks, it is doubtful that the private institutions would have been so successful.

While the increased competition engendered by privatization has led to better financial services for the economy at large, certain regions, primarily rural, have experienced reduced banking services. Privatized banks have closed most of their rural banking networks because they were unprofitable. This development has left a significant proportion of rural society with reduced access to banking services and forced them to rely on informal financial institutions for their credit needs. Since rural lending was previously conducted under regulated below market rates, some rural borrowers must now pay significantly higher interest rates.

FINANCIAL POLICY CONTEXT

In early 1982, the Bangladesh government established a program of privatization and general economic liberalization. The financial sector was partially included in this new policy direction. Before the new policies were implemented, the financial sector was almost totally controlled by the state. Six state-owned National Commercial Banks (NCBs) owned 93 percent of all bank assets, with the remainder owned by a small group of foreign banks. Outside of banking, the financial sector was and remains very limited. Other than insurance companies, non-bank sources of finance are minimal, although a nascent equity market does exist and non-bank financial institutions are growing.

Since 1981, the market share of private banks has increased sharply. By 1986, after the divestiture of two NCBs and reductions in the barriers to entry, the remaining four NCBs owned only 70 percent of bank assets. By 1988 their share was expected to fall to 50 percent. Newly established private institutions gained most of market share lost by the NCBs. The share of foreign banks has remained constant, and the two divested NCBs were small institutions.

Although greater private sector participation is being encouraged, the state continues to exercise substantial control over the financial sector. In addition to ownership of the predominant banking institutions, it greatly influences interest policies and bank lending through administered interest rates and directed credit programs to "primary sectors." The major purpose of these policies is to keep general interest costs low and to ensure that priority sectors, which include agriculture and a wide range of "politically well-connected" projects, receive credit at less-than-market rates.

For most of the directed credit programs, the Bangladesh Bank (the Bangladesh central bank) refinances loans at less-than-market rates. Even with this refinancing, however, after making provisions for bad loans, there is an estimated average negative interest rate spread of four percentage points on these directed credits. With two-thirds of the lending of the National Commercial Banks (NCBs) going to directed credit programs, it is not hard to understand why these institutions are financially troubled.

The NCBs are also required to maintain an extensive rural branch network. According to several sources, these networks are not cost effective. The banks are essentially being forced to provide a public utility type function for which they are not compensated.

Another characteristic of the Bangladesh banking environment is a slow, weak legal process for enforcing loan repayments. Even if courts do take action, it is rare for them to do so before three to four years after a bank initiates a legal process. Moreover, the regulatory structure discourages banks from taking legal action since a bank must put a loan on a non-accrual basis once legal procedures have begun. Since this classification weakens a bank's reported income, upon which bonuses are based, bank officers are averse to force loan repayment through the courts.

Finally, Bangladesh has weak regulatory and supervisory institutions and procedures. The government overseers lack qualified personnel, especially to conduct audits and other procedures to assess the financial soundness of institutions. In addition, the banking sector lacks a universal system to classify loans. Problem loans are often disguised in balance sheets because banks are loathe to take provisions against them. As a result, most of the state-owned banks report strong incomes even though they are technically bankrupt (i.e., the true value of their liabilities greatly exceeds that of their assets).

FINANCIAL POLICY REFORMS

Apart from measures to encourage greater private sector participation in the banking sector through divestiture of the smaller state-owned banks and reduced barriers to entry, few significant financial sector policy reforms have been implemented since 1981. Recently, however, authorities are recognizing the fundamental weaknesses of the banking sector and are taking tentative steps to address some of the problems.

Recent reform measures include the following:

- Relaxation of credit ceilings. Instead of using credit ceilings on individual banks as a primary monetary instrument, the central bank is attempting to implement monetary controls through interest rates, reserve requirements, and other more flexible and less discretionary mechanisms.

- The remaining state-owned banks have been encouraged to be more aggressive in collecting loan repayments. The banks have improved their performance in this regard but not enough to improve their financial position fundamentally. Politically well-connected borrowers, both private or public, still do not feel compelled to repay. NCBs are only recently willing to cut off access to credit. This poor loan recovery rate is the most important cause of the state-owned banks' poor performance.

  It should be noted that some observers believe the poor results of the NCBs' enhanced loan recovery program is due to counterproductive actions by private banks. According to these sources, many private banks willingly lend to firms and individuals that are in default to the NCBs. Since many of these creditors are connected to industrial groups and families that control most of the private banks, the perceived risk of such lending is low. In most cases, these firms and individuals have the funds to make their payments; they simply do not consider it necessary to make their payments to NCBs.

- Perhaps most importantly, a National Commission on Money, Banking and Credit was established to review and make recommendations for reforming the financial sector. Working with the IMF and the World Bank, the Commission has already made considerable progress in developing a new loan classification system that will require banks to assess their loans more realistically and take prudent banking measures to deal with problem loans. Over time, if this classification system can be enforced, it will encourage greater loan recovery efforts and better loan risk analysis. Even more far-reaching reform measures, such as the establishment of market-based interest rates and the gradual elimination of directed credit programs, are being discussed.

IMPLEMENTATION OF PRIVATIZATION

The privatization of financial institutions in Bangladesh has followed two policy paths: full and partial divestiture, and reduced barriers to entry.

Divestiture

From 1984 to 1985, the two smallest NCBs, the Pubali and the Uttara Banks, were privatized through public offerings. In 1988, the government partially divested the next smallest NCB, Rupali Bank, also through a public offering. All three of these banks were general commercial banks and provided a full range of commercial bank services. In addition, all three had extensive and costly rural branch networks.

Total Divestiture: Pubali and Uttara Banks

The two smaller banks, Pubali and Uttara, were divested near the end of a large program of privatizing an array of institutions that had been nationalized in the 1970s. Most of these enterprises were jute and textile mills. The government initially planned to privatize all enterprises formerly owned by Bangladeshis and all unprofitable state-owned enterprises. After privatizing 37 textile and jute mills in two years, opposition to the program and to the government in general began to strengthen. Populist parties and Labor unions, afraid that privatization would decrease employment and salaries, dominated the opposition. As the political strength of the Ershad government weakened, its privatization program stalled. These two NCBs were among the few enterprises outside of the jute and textile sectors that were completely divested. The privatization process for the banks, including the public offering, was conducted when opposition to privatization was mounting.

For both banks, the public offering was oversubscribed, as was the case for other public offerings of state-owned enterprises. Under the rules of the Bangladeshi stock market, where the public offerings have been placed, newly issued stock must be sold at par. Since both of these banks had many non-performing loans that were not priced to market, the antiquated accounting practices used in Bangladesh resulted in an overvaluation of the shares. The popularity of these shares was more a function of peculiarities of the Bangladeshi economy than the attractiveness of the investment. Purchasing stock shares is one of the most convenient means to launder money. By purchasing stock in cash, monies earned through black market activities are converted to legal instruments. As a result of this process, stock prices are only partially determined by the financial performance of the enterprise itself. The public offering was oversubscribed because of demand generated by laundering activities.

As a result of the public offering and significant secondary market transactions, the ownership of Pubali Bank is widespread and therefore unable to effectively influence or control bank management. Uttara Bank, however, is controlled by a large Bangladeshi industrial group which is able to oversee and supervise bank management.

Since privatization, Uttara Bank has performed well. New management has changed the bank's operating methods. It is much more commercially oriented than the NCBs, and generally conducts business like other private banks. On the other hand, Pubali Bank continues to face many of the problems of the NCBs, including poor loan recovery, strong unions that inhibit the adoption of new work practices, and a continuation of non-profitable preferred credit programs. Although Pubali Bank has not changed as rapidly as Uttara Bank, it is generally considered to be more efficient than the remaining NCBs. Nevertheless it is still in weak financial shape. Its poor condition demonstrates that although privatization can change management incentives and a bank's operating methods, without concomitant financial sector policy reforms to remove excessive government controls, both direct and indirect, and to provide sound macroeconomic conditions, privatization alone is insufficient to reform individual banks or the banking sector.

Both Pubali Bank and Uttara Bank are attempting to reduce their rural branch network and also their rural lending. The government is resisting these efforts but has no direct means to stop them. Indirectly, however, the government can hamper their activities through central bank operations and regulatory procedures. As a result, these privatized banks must reorganize more slowly than they would like in areas that contradict government policies.

Perhaps the reason that Uttara Bank has become commercially oriented more quickly is that its management is less dependent on government goodwill because its owners are a strong, independent industrial group. With this powerful group in control, the bank can resist government pressures. Rupali Bank management has no interest group to protect it and thus has been much more cautious in changing its practices and opposing the government.

Partial Divestiture: Rupali Bank

After three years of discussions, the partial divestiture of Rupali Bank, the smallest of the remaining NCBs, was implemented in the spring of 1988 through a public offering. The Rupali Bank partial divestiture was part of the Ershad government's revised privatization program. This new program resulted from a political compromise between donors who wanted a continuation of the previous stalled program and opposition interests who wanted an end to all privatization efforts. The revised program calls for only partial divestiture, up to 49 percent of an enterprise's capital, of which 15 to 20 percent is reserved for its employees. By maintaining majority control of firms, far fewer changes in management behavior are likely than if the private sector gained control of them. Although the government is officially committed to naming private sector directors from the new shareholders, the ratio of private sector to official sector representation on the board is determined by the government on a case-by-case basis.

An accelerating rate of loan defaults in the mid-1980s caused Rupali Bank to be weaker financially than the previously divested banks. Accordingly, it was restructured cosmetically through a revaluation of its fixed assets before the equity offering was issued. Since no new capital was injected by the government before the subscription, nor did the government assume any of the defaulted loans, the financial situation of the institution did not change.

As a result of Rupali Bank's poor financial situation and the generally less attractive terms of the new privatization program, demand for these shares was below expectations. Initial plans called for offering 49 percent of the bank's capital with 15 percent of total capital reserved for employees. However, as it became clear that demand for the shares was weak, the initial offering to the public was reduced from 34 percent to 20 percent. This 20 percent issue was oversubscribed and therefore hailed as a success. However, this oversubscription was possible only because a much smaller amount was offered. Employees have shown little demand for the 15 percent reserved for them. Unions want these shares to be given to employees at no cost while the government expects employees to pay. Given the strong position of unions in Bangladesh's politics, it is likely that the government will accede to the unions' demand. It should be noted that since the bank is technically close to bankruptcy, selling even 20 percent of its non-existent capital is quite an accomplishment. However, the demand for shares is not due to belief that the bank's performance will be turned around, but rather to aforementioned peculiarities of the Bangladeshi equity market. In addition, other NCBs have bought shares.

As was the case for the totally divested banks, none of the capital raised by the public offering went to the bank itself. Rather, all went to the general government coffers. This failure to use the privatization process to restructure banks is one reason why multilateral institutions are opposed to further divestitures until the public institutions are strengthened. Under the current program of partial divestiture, the government sells essentially worthless paper that has value only as long as people need a vehicle to launder their black-market funds.

Reduced Barriers to Entry

The rapid growth of newly established private banks over the past seven years demonstrates the potential of reducing barriers to entry as a mode of increasing the role of the private sector. Since 1981, when the first private local banks were established, these institutions have grown to control about 25 percent of total bank assets. In 1988 there were nine private local banks.

Although little documentation is available on how the actual process of reducing entry barriers was conducted, the results clearly illustrate the intentions of the government. As part of the government's policy to encourage greater private sector participation in the economy, it began approving a series of applications for new banks. Approval requires a full cabinet decision. In fiscal year 1982-1983, six new private banks were established. One of these was joint-venture with Arab interests, while the rest were locally controlled. Even though the policy goal was to establish private banking institutions, the government of Bangladesh has required that it hold a minimum 5 percent share in all private banks. In one of the private banks, IFIL, the government holds a 40 percent share.

Since the first six banks were established in 1982-1983, one other bank, an Islamic bank, followed in 1987. With the two privatized state-owned banks, the local private banking sector includes nine institutions. The fact that none of them have failed indicates that as a group they are doing relatively well. According to several observers, most are quite profitable and are growing. However, due to the industry's poor reporting and accounting practices, an accurate picture of an individual bank's financial condition is not available.

Private banks have prospered in Bangladesh primarily because of the poor banking practices and the required unprofitable lending of the state-owned banks that dominate the market. The private banks, unlike the NCBs, cannot be forced to lend under the preferred credit programs. Moreover, the private banks conduct more vigorous loan repayment programs. According to several sources, these include sending out "thugs" to recover payments. More importantly, creditors who do not repay are cut off from any further lending. Political connections do not play as important a role in lending decisions. Private banks lend to relatively low-risk, well-established private firms and individuals. The higher risk lending is left to the NCBs.

In addition, unlike the NCBs, the private banks match their deposits with their lending needs. The NCBs, following official policy, attempt to mobilize deposits as an objective in and of itself, regardless of their need for funds. As might be expected, the NCBs have excess liquidity. With only a small interbank market and a small government security market due to the absence of a sizeable fiscal deficit, there are few instruments or markets in which to place these funds. The NCBs have invested some of their excess liquidity in the privatized banks. Because of the excess deposits, the NCBs have no cash flow problem, even though they are technically bankrupt. When deposit growth ebbs, however, the cash flow situation will also deteriorate, bringing on a financial crisis. Hopefully, reform efforts can proceed quickly enough to avoid such a crisis.

Most of the private banks are either controlled or closely associated with a large family-run industrial group. For some groups, the primary purpose of the bank is to serve as a financing instrument for other enterprises in the group or connected to the family. Because of these connections, the risk of non-payment is low, as long as the group is committed to the viability of the bank. However, it is possible for the bank to serve as a source of funds to bail out failing enterprises. In this scenario, the interests of depositors could be threatened.

RESULTS

Over the seven year period since the Ershad government began its financial sector privatization policies, the financial sector has grown and deepened by most measures. Credit to the private sector expanded from 6.2 percent of GDP in 1981 to 16.7 percent in 1987. Similarly, the ratio of M2 (a broad monetary aggregate) to GDP, the most widely used indicator of financial deepening, grew from 20 percent to 25 percent. Finally, the ability of the financial sector to mobilize resources also expanded sharply. The ratio of time deposits to GDP rose from 11 percent of GDP in 1981 to 15 percent in 1987.

Although much of the growth of the financial sector is due to the generally sound macroeconomic policies implemented over this period, policies to encourage a greater role for the private sector in financial activities played an important role. Private enterprises have taken advantage of profit opportunities, which have fueled their expansion. While part of the financial sector's growth results from the public sector's program of expanding financial services in the rural sector, most of the growth, especially on the lending side, has come from private financial institutions.

While the expansion of the financial sector is helpful for economic development, it must be remembered that in Bangladesh this expansion happened concurrently with the development of serious structural problems in the financial sector. If these problems are not addressed soon, the expansion could be reversed very rapidly. Privatization has helped the financial sector expand and provide services to the most buoyant areas of the economy, but it does not directly address the fundamental problems of the sector. These must be attacked through financial policy reforms and institutional changes at the NCBs.

By providing effective competition to the NCBs, however, the private financial sector is contributing to the momentum for needed, fundamental structural reforms. Through superior management and greater freedom from government interference, private banks have taken away most of the profitable business from the NCBs, leaving them with only unprofitable government-mandated lending. Previously, NCBs could operate inefficiently and conduct unprofitable lending and still stay solvent because they had a cushion of profitable lending to the private sector. In short, the government allowed taxation through the financial sector of some elements of society to provide subsidies to others. With the advent of private bank competition, this flawed policy became inoperable because the "taxes" became much harder to collect. In addition, the costs of the subsidies (non-payment of loans, losses due to mandated lending at less-than-market rates, etc.) have increased to the point that the government has decided to try to curtail them. In the political process to reform the system, the rise of the private sector provides a powerful interest group in support of market-based financial sector reform.

Although private banks provide effective competition to the NCBs, there is considerable evidence of collusion to limit competition. For example, in the few cases where some interest rate levels have been liberalized, the rates have gone almost immediately to the mandated ceiling at every bank, even when lending at the previous lower administered rate was clearly profitable. Whether collusion would continue if there were greater liberalization that allowed for competition in many more areas is unclear. However, the fact that collusion seems to be taking place gives substantial ammunition to the opponents of additional financial sector liberalization.

LESSONS AND APPLICATIONS

The primary lesson of the Bangladeshi financial sector privatization efforts is that reducing barriers to entry is an effective means of developing the role of the private sector. These new institutions can develop new management styles and corporate cultures without the wrenching changes that are required to reform an existing institution. Moreover, their success can serve as a model for managers in existing troubled institutions. Finally, the political obstacles to this mode of privatization are much less than to the transfer of existing institutions from the public to the private sector. Obviously, for this strategy to work, there must be areas where these new institutions can operate profitably. If all financial services are controlled such that it is impossible to earn profits, no new banks will be established. Accordingly, some semblance of financial liberalization must be completed before this strategy can be implemented.

The Bangladeshi experience also illustrates that the successful selling of shares does not mean that privatization is successful. The object of privatization is not to market shares, but rather to improve the efficiency of an enterprise by changing ownership and thereby changing management incentives. Partial divestitures that leave control of the institution with the government will not accomplish this goal unless minority shareholders can influence management. Moreover, the Bangladeshi experience also demonstrates that share prices even in a competitive market do not necessarily reflect their true value. Small and thin equity markets in developing countries can be strongly influenced by non-financial factors. The nature of equity markets should be analyzed closely before public offerings are issued.

Chile:
Innovative Bank Divestiture

SUMMARY

Financial institutions in Chile have experienced two waves of privatization. The first wave was implemented in the mid-1970s when the Pinochet regime came to power and returned twenty commercial banks, nationalized under the previous Allende government, to the private sector. In the early 1980s, when the private banks became burdened with bad loans and escalating interest payments on external funds, the government stepped in and regained ownership and control. These banks were then "reprivatized" in the mid-1980s.

The first group of privatizations is instructive in "what not to do." The extensive interlocking ownership between large business groups and the banks that resulted from the hasty privatizations led to unsound lending decisions, which the weak regulatory framework and supervisory system was incapable of detecting and preventing. While it is too soon to pass definitive judgment, initial signs indicate that the second series of privatizations, which utilized several innovative privatization techniques, can serve positively to guide other nations seeking to reform and invigorate their financial markets. In particular, the "popular capitalism" method of facilitating widespread share ownership by offering no-interest financing holds promise for further use.

THE FIRST PRIVATIZATION WAVE

The Financial Policy Context

Chilean financial institutions have gone through five stages in the last twenty years: nationalization, liberalization, development of close ties with industrial groups, direct state control, and reprivatization and deregulation.

Prior to the first privatization wave in 1974-1975, the Chilean financial system was characterized by complete government ownership of all financial intermediaries. Interest rate controls resulted in negative real rates for lending and saving. A plethora of targeted credit programs channeled investment funds to state-owned companies and high-priority government projects. Banking deposits were not insured, but widespread belief was that the government would intervene if needed to safeguard deposits.

Financial Policy Reform

During the mid-1970s, the Pinochet government, following the advice of the "Chicago school of economics," undertook a sweeping set of initiatives to liberalize the economy. The government relaxed tariff barriers, tightened monetary policy to rein in inflation, liberalized the financial system by eliminating interest rate controls, and embarked on a massive wave of privatizations. During that decade, the government also experimented with regulatory reform by granting banks and other financial institutions greater operating freedom.

As one of their first financial liberalization measures, the government abolished interest rate ceilings on both lending and deposits for thrifts, giving rise to a new class of financial institutions. In 1976, 26 new thrifts were established. One year later, interest rate ceilings on commercial bank deposits and loans were abolished. Interest rates paid on peso deposits and other peso-denominated assets increased dramatically. From 1979 to 1982, interest rates on peso deposits earned an average of 20 percentage points more than the London Interbank Offer Rate (LIBOR). These high interest rates triggered a massive inflow of capital; the banks borrowed at the relatively low rates abroad and re-lent funds at higher rates.

The government's decision in June 1979, to abandon the "crawling peg" exchange rate regime and set the exchange rate at 39 Chilean pesos to the U.S. dollar, fueled the foreign borrowing. Banks moved quickly to increase their foreign indebtedness and take advantage of the artificially low peso. Foreign borrowing increased further in 1980 when limits on bank borrowing from overseas markets were abolished.

The government also liberalized laws regulating bank ownership. A 1974 law limited bank ownership by individuals to 1.5 percent and by firms and organizations to 3 percent. In the prevailing lax supervisory environment, the law was not enforced and was then rescinded in 1978. Barriers to entry by foreign banks were removed, and they flocked to the country. In 1979 alone, 8 foreign banks opened in Chile, tripling the number of foreign banks from 4 to 12.

In an additional liberalization move, the government ended targeted credit programs. This extremely important measure changed banks from passive funnels of rediscounted Central Bank funds to preferred sectors to active intermediaries. They began attracting private funds by offering attractive deposit rates and lending those funds at market rates to enterprises with the potential to make a profit and repay the loan.

Beginning in May 1976, the Central Bank started paying market rates on bank reserves. The government then reduced reserve requirements, which reduced bank costs by increasing their pool of loanable funds. The reserve requirement for banks was reduced to 10 percent for sight deposits and 4 percent for time deposits.

Implementation of Privatization

Financial market liberalization in the 1970s was accompanied by a rash of privatizations as the staunchly anti-socialist military government moved to sell the firms nationalized by the previous government. In 1973-1974, 92 firms, including 11 banks, were sold to private interests. An additional 350 firms were returned to their previous owners.

Because of political concerns over foreign ownership, foreign firms were prohibited from buying the Chilean companies. The only source of sufficient local capital to buy the banks was the "grupos," large Chilean-owned business conglomerates. The conglomerates were interested in buying the banks to acquire bank capital to purchase other state-owned businesses being offered for sale. In a financing scheme that became known as "the bicycle," the banks lent funds to the conglomerates to purchase SOEs, with the shares of the businesses being purchased serving as collateral. The result of the flurry of buying activity in 1973-1974 was that each major conglomerate purchased a bank which then lent the conglomerate funds to purchase additional businesses.

Results

Initially, the liberalization and privatization brought about several economic benefits. Financial market liberalization resulted in rapid growth and proliferation in the number and type of institutions operating in Chile (see Table A.1). Lifting interest rate controls in 1976 resulted in the creation of a new class of savings and loan institutions, the finance companies (*financieras*). As one knowledgeable observer reports,

> The volume and diversification of government and Central Bank papers in the market increased noticeably; the range and number of mutual funds increased manifold; businesses began to issue signif-icant amounts of commercial paper which were intermediated by depository institutions, stock exchanges and mutual funds; the insurance business expanded its list of products; consumer credit offered by financial institutions expanded noticeably. (Ludens, as reported in Velasco, p. 8.)

Table A.1
Chile: Growth in Financial Systems as a Result of Liberalization

	1974	1975	1976	1977	1978	1979	1980	1981	1982	1983	1984
Total number of banks & finance companies	<u>21</u>	<u>21</u>	<u>46</u>	<u>39</u>	<u>47</u>	<u>54</u>	<u>56</u>	<u>54</u>	<u>49</u>	<u>45</u>	<u>45</u>
Domestic banks	20	20	18	18	22	24	25	23	21	19	19
Foreign banks	1	1	2	3	4	12	13	18	19	19	19
Finance companies	--	--	26	18	21	18	18	13	9	7	7

Source: Andres Velasco, "Liberalization, Crisis, Intervention: The Chilean Financial System, 1975," Central Banking Department, International Monetary Fund, July 21, 1988, unpublished manuscript.

The wave of liberalization and privatization did not appear to have increased the savings rate. The average savings rate for the liberalization decade, 1974-1983, was 10.7 percent, which was actually slightly lower than the 12.6 rate experienced from 1966-1973. In short, the strategy produced only shifts in asset holding rather than true incentives for capital formation.

The decline in government regulation and the return of firms to private ownership did spur private investment, at least until 1981 when a recession cooled the incentives to invest (see Table A.2). From 1975 to 1981, gross private domestic capital formation as a percentage of GDP increased from 4.6 to 15.6 percent. At the same time, government capital formation decreased as the government attempted to reduce the fiscal

Table A.2
Chile: Gross Domestic Capital Formation
(as a percentage of GDP)

	Gross Domestic Capital Formation		
	Private	Public	Total
1960-65	3.8	10.5	14.3
1966-70	4.7	11.3	16.0
1971-73	-0.9	12.4	11.5
1974	8.4	12.8	21.2
1975	4.6	8.5	13.1
1976	7.4	5.4	12.8
1977	7.7	7.7	14.4
1978	11.6	6.2	17.8
1979	12.6	5.2	17.8
1980	15.6	5.4	21.0
1981	15.6	5.1	20.7
1982	...	...	11.3
1983	...	...	9.8
1984	...	...	13.6
1985	...	...	13.7

Source: <u>Cuentas Nacionales de Chile, 1960-1983</u>, Direccion de Politica Financiera, Central Bank of Chile, as quoted in Andes Velasco, "Liberalization, Crisis, Intervention: The Chilean Financial System, 1975, 1965," Central Banking Department, International Monetary Fund, unpublished manuscript, July 21, 1988.

deficit. Thus one result of the liberalization was that domestic investment as a percentage of GDP increased slightly, and the composition of investment shifted dramatically to the private sector.

While the measures resulted in unprecedented financial institution widening and deepening, in hindsight it appears that many of the institutions were unprepared to operate in the unrestricted environment. Widespread bank failures resulted when the economy entered a recessionary period in the late 1970s. The bank failures were brought on by excessive concentration of bank loan portfolios, the newness of operating in a free market environment, the dearth of skills necessary to operate successfully in that environment, and a lack of supervision. Another important cause was the sudden increase in nonperforming loans due to excessive foreign borrowing, the devaluation of the peso, and falling commodities prices.

Interlocking ownership between groups of large industrial companies and the banks led to excessive risk taking as the banks channeled large quantities of funds to their own enterprises. In 1981, loans to companies that were partial owners of the banks reached an average of 21 percent of the loan portfolio in the five largest banks. They were 46 percent of the portfolio of Banco de Santiago, the nation's largest private bank.

Other destabilizing influences also contributed to the financial crash. In 1982-1983, the prices of Chile's main exports, especially copper, collapsed. The financial condition of the banks' clients was weakened by high domestic real interest rates, which averaged 77 percent from 1975 to 1982, and by rising interest rates abroad. The number of corporate bankruptcies rose from 2 in 1978 to 15 in 1980 and 75 in 1982. The sudden, large devaluations of the peso beginning in 1982 multiplied the value in pesos of the dollar-denominated debt obligations of both banks and firms.

THE SECOND PRIVATIZATION WAVE

The Financial Policy Context

For the reasons just cited, Chile entered a severe recession in the early 1980s. It is important to note that Chile's macroeconomic difficulties did not affect all the banks equally. Management capabilities at the individual bank level were crucial in determining the banks' ability to withstand the external pressures. The government-owned, conservatively managed Banco del Estado was affected only marginally, as were the foreign banks operating in Chile.

With few exceptions, however, the locally-owned Chilean banks entered a period of extreme financial weakness and instability. From 1981 to 1983, the Chilean government intervened in or liquidated a number of financial institutions: ten commercial banks, including the nation's two largest commercial banks, and five finance companies, which were on the brink of collapse. The Chilean government liquidated three banks, nationalized five, and appointed overseers to two more.

Financial Policy Reforms

Many of the current capital markets laws and regulations were motivated by the Chilean financial crisis of 1982. The overriding goal of new regulations and stronger supervision is to prevent the difficulties of the early 1980s, to the extent possible. For the most part, the regulations appear to have struck an appropriate balance between the under-regulation and over-regulation of the past.

The most important pieces of legislation affecting financial markets are the Capital Markets Law (Law 18.045 of 1981) and the General Banking Law (Law 18.576 of 1986). The three basic tenets of Chilean capital markets laws are nondiscrimination, transparency, and tax neutrality. Nondiscrimination means that local and foreign firms must be treated alike. Transparency means that transactions are to be visible and closely scrutinized for compliance with laws and regulations. The Superintendency of Banks is required to publish information on the nature and quality of financial institutions' assets three times each year. Lastly, the tax structure is designed to minimize bias either for or against debt as opposed to equity finance, thus allowing financing options to be evaluated on their own merits and not on their tax consequences.

In 1981, the government adopted measures to limit bank exposure to individual companies and subsidiaries. It prohibited banks from accepting stock as loan collateral, thus addressing a key cause of financial instability.

The government implemented a formal deposit insurance program in 1983. The insurance coverage was gradually decreased. In June 1986, deposit insurance was granted only to banks that met minimum capital requirements, upon application. By 1989, only small depositors were insured and only 90 percent coverage of small savings accounts was guaranteed by the government.

The government also tightened bank supervision by reorganizing the supervisory functions. The Central Bank and three Superintendencies regulate the many institutions that make up the Chilean financial markets.

The Superintendency of Banks and Financial Institutions is the governmental organization charged with regulating and supervising commercial, development and investment banks, thrifts, and credit cooperatives. The Superintendency is organized into four departments—Accounting, Supervision, Research, and Legal Counsel—and employs 150 professionals. The supervisory body requests and reviews quarterly statistical information on the institutions it supervises, verifies compliance with regulations, and assesses the quality of the loan portfolios. A second regulatory body, the Superintendency of Securities and Insurance Companies, oversees the stock exchange, securities dealers, brokers, mutual funds, and insurance companies. The third agency, the Superintendency of Pension Fund Administrators (AFPs) oversees only AFPs.

Since the 1981-1983 recession, Chile has worked to improve the record-keeping of financial institutions. The results are impressive. Disclosure and reporting requirements in Chile are the most comprehensive in Latin America and have made an important contribution to high quality supervision and confidence in the system. Accurate statistics are available on a timely basis for overseers as well as policymakers and researchers.

Implementation of Privatization

Objectives: In keeping with its philosophy of a "social market economy" (Doctrina de una Economia Social del Mercado), the government made plans to sell the banks to the private sector. According to official government publications, the rationale for the privatizations was as follows. First, the government must respect private property and cement property rights as firmly as possible in laws. It must allow free exercise of private productive activities and let the market assign resources through supply, demand, and price. In sum, the Pinochet regime firmly believed that the state must seek a subsidiary role to private enterprise in directing the economy.

The privatization had several secondary objectives as well. Through privatization, the Chilean government was seeking a wide distribution of state-owned wealth. This redistribution would not only result in a more just ownership of wealth but also would serve as a barrier to future excesses of political and economic power by the State.

Privatization Step 1: Set time limit for return of nationalized enterprises. Soon after intervening in the troubled institutions, the government announced that the banks would be returned to the private sector by

December 31, 1986. The last bank was returned nearly on schedule, in April 1987.

Privatization Step 2: Improve asset quality. In order to return the government banks to private hands, the government first needed to make them attractive investments. Bad loan portfolios were the key obstacle to the banks' financial health. The Central Bank agreed to save the banks by purchasing the nonperforming loans from the troubled institutions with an agreement that the banks would divert future dividend payments to repurchase their loan portfolios. The Central Bank bought, at book value, nonperforming loans in amounts up to 3.5 times each bank's capital base in return for Central Bank notes. The banks were required to divert future dividends on common stock to the Central Bank up to the point where they had repurchased the entire loan portfolio. Banks are allowed to issue preferred shares, which can pay 50 percent of normal dividends. Through this mechanism, the Central Bank acquired $3 billion in nonperforming loans.

Privatization Step 3: Use creative financing mechanisms if necessary. Once the balance sheets were improved, the Central Bank utilized another innovative tool, which they named "popular capitalism," to encourage the public to buy shares in the banks. The Central Bank offered 15-year loans for up to UF2,000 at zero percent real interest to small investors who bought shares. Only citizens who were current on their taxes were eligible for the preferential financing. A total of 400,000 people took advantage of the no-interest funds and purchased $400 million of shares in the two leading banks, Banco de Chile and Banco de Santiago. The Central Bank estimates that it managed to recapitalize the banks at a cost of only 8–10 percent of what it would have cost to liquidate them.

Privatization Step 4: The sale. Lacking securities underwriters, the government announced that CORFO, the Chilean National Development Corporation, would buy any unpurchased increase in the capital stock. The government would in essence trade the emergency credits granted in the previous years for equity. However, the government ownership would not last indefinitely. CORFO was required to sell at least 20 percent of its shares each year. Thus, within five years the government would divest all its shares in the banks. Since the sales were fully subscribed, it was not necessary for CORFO to acquire any shares.

Results

Too few years have passed since the privatizations and financial reforms were implemented to pass definitive judgment on their efficacy.

However, it appears that competition among privately owned financial institutions in Chile has resulted in a wide variety of instruments for savers. Individuals and firms with excess funds can choose from instruments with fixed and variable interest rates and with varying maturities and degrees of safety. Banks in Chile are still recovering from the crash and have yet to attain full financial soundness. One can tentatively conclude, however, that Chile is approaching an appropriate balance between government control and regulation, which limits capital market innovation and development, and hands-off policies, which allow banks and related corporations to pursue high-risk strategies that destabilize the entire financial sector.

As Table A.3 indicates, the Chilean financial markets consist of a large number of private institutions competing with one another. Of the five types of institutions—official institutions, commercial banks, investment banks, development banks, and other financial intermediaries—commercial banks are by far the most important player. Sixteen locally owned banks and 20 foreign banks serve the Chilean market.

The Chilean government has limited its participation in the financial sector to a few key functions in which government is the logical, appropriate player. Only one bank, the large Banco del Estado, is still owned by the government. As the largest bank in Chile, it serves the financial needs of government entities and holds Treasury deposits.

In contrast to its earlier, wide-ranging responsibilities, the Chilean Central Bank is now charged with issuing currency, implementing monetary policy along guidelines set out by the Monetary Council, serving as lender of last resort, and implementing debt-to-equity conversions. The Bank makes use of the same three tools used by the U.S. Federal Reserve to control the money supply: reserve requirements, open market operations, and a rediscount facility. Since 1982, the Bank has been called upon numerous times to provide emergency credits to rescue banks and financieras and their depositors.

While the government has divested nearly all its financial holdings, it still owns a number of companies in other sectors. CORFO is the publicly-owned holding company for the state-owned enterprises. CORFO provides low-cost loans to its holdings, utilizing profits from its surplus-generating enterprises and multilateral development bank funds. Government enterprises generate approximately one-quarter of Chile's GDP. In contrast to those in many countries, most of the government-owned businesses in Chile are profitable. Together, they contributed 9.1 percent of government budget revenues in the mid-1980s.

Table A.3
Chile: Capital Markets Profile—November 1988

Capital Markets Institutions	Number of Firms	Number of Government-Owned Firms	Regulated By
OFFICIAL INSTITUTIONS			
Central Bank	1	1	na
Banco del Estado	1	1	B
COMMERCIAL BANKS	36	0	B
Locally-owned	16	0	B
Foreign-owned	20	0	B
INVESTMENT BANKS			
Soc. Financieras	4	0	B
Agentes de Valores	25	0	S
DEVELOPMENT BANKS			
Corfo	1	1	E
OTHER			
Stock Exchanges	1	0	S
Mutual Funds	5	0	S
Leasing Companies	13	0	S
Pension Funds	12	0	A
Insurance Companies	17	0	S
Savings and Loans	4	0	B
Credit Cooperatives	2	0	B

na   Not applicable.
A   Superintendency of AFPs.
B   Superintendency of Banks and Financial Institutions.
E   Ministry of Economy.
S   Superintendency of Securities and Insurance.

SOURCES: Chilean Central Bank and Superintendency Monthly Bulletins;
           SRI Calculations

Even with the extensive private ownership and competition in the Chilean banking system, investment banking in Chile is fairly undeveloped. Four "financieras" and 25 securities brokers underwrite share issues and trade in public and private bonds and notes. They also offer cash management, financial advice, and merger and acquisition services.

Chile is one of the few countries in the world with a private pension system. Since 1981, employees and self-employed individuals have had to channel 10 percent of total wages to private pension funds (Administradoras de Fondos de Pensiones—AFPs), which create personal retirement accounts and invest the funds in government securities and low-risk bonds and shares. The top three pension funds all have substantial foreign ownership. In 1986, Bankers Trust purchased a 40 percent share in Provida, S.A., the largest pension fund, using pesos obtained through a debt-to-equity conversion. Aetna owns 50 percent of the second largest pension fund, Santa Maria, and the American Insurance Group (AIG) has a substantial participation in La Interamericana, the third largest fund.

As a result of financial liberalization, Chilean banks offer positive real interest rates to savers. Real short-term (90–365 day) deposit rates averaged 4.1 percent in 1986; lending rates on the same maturity averaged 7.7 percent. The annual real rate of return on the fixed-income instruments traded on the stock exchange averaged 5.1 percent.

LESSONS AND APPLICATIONS

The two Chilean experiences in privatization offer several lessons for other countries seeking to reduce the role of government direction in the economy and specifically in the financial sector. The first lesson, drawn from Chile's privatization of the 1970s, is that hasty private sales of banks to large local corporations should be avoided. This warning is especially true if the regulatory framework is weak. Although initially such concentrations of capital may seem to be the only available local capital, the negative effects of tightly interlocking bank/corporate directorates can include skewed, concentrated loan portfolios with the potential to undermine financial stability. The Chilean experience served as a poignant illustration that while rapid privatization to large local interests meets pressing short-term political needs to move forward on privatization, it may undermine the entire privatization strategy in the long term.

Another lesson offered by the Chilean experience is the importance of a strong regulatory framework. Government oversight was extremely deficient following the first wave of privatizations, and it did not detect or prevent the ensuing financial crash. The critical components of effective government supervision of financial institutions are:

- Standardized accounting practices and adequate audit capabilities to insure accurate and timely estimates of company performance and loan quality.
- Sufficient quantity and quality of regulatory personnel.
- Development of a series of prudential regulations and ratios, and *strict monitoring of compliance with prudential ratios and effective penalties for noncompliance*.

The Chilean experience also illustrates the need for controlling growth in the financial sector. The rapid emergence of dozens of new financial institutions strained the Chilean management capacity beyond what it could handle, and inexperienced managers' decisions contributed to the financial crash. Competition and freedom of entry are critical components of a functioning financial system, but adequate capital requirements and strict experience requirements for top management should accompany the liberalization of a financial system.

Several positive lessons can also be drawn from the Chilean privatizations. First, Chile's "popular capitalism" is an impressive example of a way to increase share ownership in the national economy and rapidly recapitalize a financial institution. The mechanism proved to be cost-effective, compared to other recapitalization methods, and also very popular from a political standpoint. Widespread ownership is one of the strongest deterrents to future nationalization attempts. Facilitating share purchase by lower and middle class individuals is perhaps the only way to interest these groups in participating in privatization.

Some observers of the Chilean financial system are concerned that the nation has now gone too far in the direction of disaggregated ownership. They argue that the tens of thousands of small shareholders in Chile's commercial banks do not have the interest or knowledge in bank operations needed to provide effective oversight of the Board of Directors.

To reduce this concern, large local corporations could be approached to serve as lead, but still minority, owners of newly-privatized banks. A locally owned "grupo" could be approached with an offer of from five to twenty percent of bank shares, enough to assure that the corporation has a strong interest in the bank's profitability but not enough to create corruptive links or force biased lending decisions. Unfortunately, most large businesses in developing countries prefer to hold a controlling interest or not be involved. However, if a sufficiently attractive offer is made, perhaps some businesses would accept minority participation. The presence of a substantial owner would improve shareholder oversight. In the case of a bank with a doubtful asset base and uncertain future profitability, a share purchase by a well-known local business would increase the level of confidence in the quality of the investment and improve the prospects for a successful share offering.

Second, Chile demonstrated that even banks with large portfolios of nonperforming assets can be successfully privatized if the government first takes appropriate measures to improve the balance sheets. By temporarily assuming the nonperforming assets, the Central Bank increased the attractiveness of the banks to private investors without accepting the full burden and cost of the bad loans. In essence, the Chilean government created a mechanism to share the responsibility for past poor lending conditions and unforeseen external economic forces between the banks' owners and the government.

Guinea:
Creation of a Private Banking Sector

SUMMARY

In the mid-1980s, several years after the death of Sekou Toure, the founder of the Guinean state, the nation's new leaders began a radical program to transform the socialist economy developed during Toure's twenty-year reign. The new leaders have attempted to convert the moribund socialist economic structure into a dynamic, market-based system, with the state continuing to play a major role. This transformation program has included the closing of many state-owned enterprises, allowing private markets to allocate and distribute most goods, and a general opening of the economy to foreign markets.

A key element of this radical restructuring was the establishment and development of a new banking system, in which all the leading banks were joint ventures between French multinational banks and the Guinean state. The previous system performed banking services in name only. Rather than serving as institutions to intermediate financial claims and liabilities and to clear payments, the banks under the old regime served as credit dispensing agencies for public enterprises and as vehicles for monetary creation. This previous system, which was notoriously corrupt, was closed on December 26, 1985, and replaced on January 6, 1986, with the establishment of three joint-venture banks. The opening of the new banks was combined with other financial sector reforms to give the new system a solid economic framework upon which to build. The reforms included the creation of a new currency and a massive devaluation to bring the new currency closer to a realistic level. Since the establishment of the first three joint-venture banks, a fourth one has been established.

Compared to the dismal state of the previous banking system, the new private system is a vast improvement. Credit, although short term, is available to the private sector, and a relatively efficient payments mechanism is operating. However, due primarily to a series of structural problems, the new system has failed to mobilize domestic savings effectively and is not profitable, according to most sources. Problems include: the lack of a legal system or even clear property rights through which one can enforce contracts and force repayment; inappropriate monetary and financial policies that overvalue the currency and keep all but the shortest-term interest rates negative in real terms; and the lack of experienced Guinean bankers, forcing the new banks to employ highly-paid expatriates at virtually all top and even mid-level management positions, leading to high operating costs.

Even with the current difficulties, the Guinean experience demonstrates that a new private banking system can be developed very quickly. Foreign involvement is the key factor in the quick establishment of these institutions. However, the Guinean experience also shows that to develop an efficient system, appropriate financial and legal policies must simultaneously be established and enforced. Without them no financial system can operate effectively.

FINANCIAL POLICY CONTEXT

The banking sector of the pre-reform economy was moribund and performed few, if any, banking services. As would be expected in a socialist state, all banking institutions except for one small Islamic bank were state owned and operated. Although these institutions were called banks, they were banks in name only. Rather than intermediating financial claims and liabilities, these institutions served primarily as credit dispensing agents to public agencies and as conduits for monetary creation to finance the large government deficit. Theoretically, these "banks" accepted deposits, but almost none were placed voluntarily. The majority of deposits were composed of required deposits from public employees and the deposits of public agencies. (Once the "banks" were closed, a large number of voluntary deposits were "found." According to most sources, these voluntary deposits were created by corrupt banking officials to obtain money from the government during the closure process.)

In addition to providing few banking services, the banks were notoriously inefficient and corrupt. Not only did this tradition make their closure costly but it also left the country with no experienced bankers who could be trusted to manage any banking operation efficiently or honestly. As a result, many private Guineans became hesitant to use banks or any other formal financial institution to meet their financial service needs. Similarly, those who did use these institutions had little experience about the need to repay loans on time or at all.

FINANCIAL POLICY REFORMS

The joint-venture banking institutions were part of a coordinated program to establish quickly a new, more efficient banking and financial system. Guinean financial planners and their advisors understood that without changes in the underlying macroeconomic and monetary structure of the economy, a new banking system would not be able to operate effectively. Accordingly, the same day the new banks were formally established, a new currency, the Guinean franc, was issued. Its foreign exchange value was several times less than the overvalued previous currency. In addition, weekly foreign exchange auctions were established to set the price and to allocate foreign exchange freely.

More liberal financial policies, consistent with a system of independent and competitive banking institutions, were also established. Rather than a system of administered interest rates, interest rate ceilings were established. Although this system gave banks flexibility in setting their credit policies, ceilings have been set below the inflation rate, which has discouraged deposits except those of a very short-term nature.

While these policy reforms represent a vast improvement over the previous regime, they have not gone far enough to establish the conditions needed for a dynamic financial sector. In addition to maintaining negative real interest rates, the Central Bank has intervened in the auctions to keep the rate of currency devaluation below the rate of inflation, and inflation continues to be high, running at an annual rate of approximately 20 percent. Perhaps most importantly, little has been done to establish an effective legal system or to clearly demarcate property rights. Guinea's socialist and village communal traditions inhibit the formulation of individual property rights necessary for functioning private markets.

IMPLEMENTATION OF PRIVATIZATION

On December 23, 1985, the old "banking" system was closed. After a two-week bank holiday, three new joint-venture banking institutions were formally established on January 6, 1986. All three of the new banks were formed as joint ventures between French multinational banks and the Guinean state. The government owns a slight majority of the capital of two of the banks. As part of a World Bank loan, which provided most of the funds for the government's participation in these banks, the state is committed to selling its share to private Guinean interests by 1991. However, it is unlikely that the state will be able to meet this commitment because the banks are currently unprofitable and local private interests lack sufficient investment capital.

Guinean leaders understood early that the creation of a viable and dynamic financial sector capable of efficiently allocating financial resources was a prerequisite for the successful liberalization of their economy. After rejecting the possibility of reforming the existing state-owned institutions (because of their poor financial condition, corrupt and inefficient corporate cultures, and absence of competent managers), a decision was made to close the existing banks and invite foreign banks to participate in establishing new institutions.

Since a viable financial system was considered a prerequisite for other necessary structural reforms, there was great urgency to establish the new system quickly. Banks from several countries, including the United States, were invited to negotiate with the government to establish joint ventures. However, only three French banks, all of which have extensive African banking networks and which were formally involved in Guinea before independence, successfully completed negotiations. Each bank negotiated separate "convention speciales," or operating agreements, that specified tax advantages, repatriation allowances, and special expatriate employment privileges. Negotiations were conducted quickly to ensure that the banks could open by January 6, 1986, when the new system was established.

Although the government owns a majority of their capital, the banks are effectively controlled by the expatriate managers who fill all top and most mid-level positions. Through these managers, the foreign banks are able to set policies at the institutions. Moreover, their "convention speciales" give them significant flexibility with financial flows, which allows them to run these banks essentially as branch offices. Government influence on the banking sector operates through the setting of financial and monetary policy, not through ownership rights. With effective control and their extensive experience operating similar operations in West Africa, the French banks had little difficulty in establishing these Guinean joint-venture operations. Their difficulties have come from attempting to operate profitably in a problem-ridden financial and legal environment.

The most troublesome phase of the implementation of a "private" banking system came from the closing of the old banking system. The problems did not arise from any loss of services, since the old banks provided none, but rather from the costs of closure. In closing the banks, it appears that bank officials created fictitious deposits, which the government is now attempting to cover.

Many of the old banks' assets were loans to public agencies. Most of these were poorly documented and are uncollectible in any case due to the poor financial condition of these agencies. After marking these loans down to their true value, the old banks were left with liabilities of more than double their assets. The absence of competent and honest banking officials to oversee the closure of the banks contributed significantly to the cost of the operation. In addition, the decision to close the old system quickly also contributed to the cost; there was no time to hire a sufficient number of qualified, objective experts for a long enough period to ensure that the accounting was done correctly and with adequate safeguards.

RESULTS

On several levels, the Guinean program to develop a private banking system has been quite successful. Three joint-venture institutions were established at the beginning of the program in early 1986, and a fourth joint venture was established in 1988. These four privately operated institutions, along with the smaller Islamic bank that dates to the Toure regime, provide banking services far superior to those of the old system. Short-term credit is now available for commerce, especially external trade, and a relatively efficient payments mechanism now exists. Credit is allocated primarily on the basis of ability to pay, not on political connections, even though one's ability to pay itself is often a function of the latter.

Although the new system is able to provide adequate financial services for the Guinean economy, it has not been able to mobilize financial resources significantly, nor, apparently, have the banks yet been able to operate profitably. The lack of profitability did not seem to inhibit a fourth French bank from establishing a bank in Guinea, indicating that some close observers believe that the market has considerable potential or that the banks are hiding their local gains and taking their profits elsewhere through the manipulation of financial accounts.

Both of these shortfalls are due primarily to continued serious structural and policy weaknesses. Under current macroeconomic and financial policies, through which interest rates are negative and the exchange rate is overvalued, there is little incentive for savers to invest in local financial instruments, primarily bank deposits and local currency. Rather, the incentive is to invest in real assets (goods and real estate) or in foreign exchange, preferably overseas wherever interest rates are highest. Under these conditions, it is difficult for financial deepening (an increase in the value of financial assets as a percentage of total output) to occur. Furthermore, banks can do little by themselves to encourage financial resource mobilization. Opening more branches would reduce transaction costs, but not enough to overcome the disincentives to use the financial system for anything but a payments vehicle.

The unprofitability of the banks is attributable to the high default rate on credits and very high operating costs. It is reported that 30-40 percent of the bank loans made since the creation of the banks in 1986 are in default. The poor payment record is a result of the country's lack of experience with banking practices, that is, the need to repay loans (and if possible on time). Even more importantly, the bad debt rate is worsened by the lack of a legal system to enforce contracts and property rights. Indeed, property rights themselves are not clearly defined. With no means to enforce payments, banks can do little to collect loans except to cut off a customer's further access to credit.

The banks' high operating costs are due to the need to employ highly paid expatriates at all top management and most mid-level management positions. Some observers have criticized the banks for this practice. But they have little choice if they are to operate even moderately efficient and honest operations, since the old system generated almost no competent bank management. Since banks could reduce operating costs by employing Guineans, one would expect the percentage of local managers to increase over time.

LESSONS

The Guinean experience provides several lessons on privatization. On the positive side, a viable private banking system can be developed from the ground up very quickly, if experienced foreign banks are allowed to play the management role. When time is of the essence, this foreign-bank-based strategy is an appropriate approach to privatization. However, it is an expensive strategy. Not only will these institutions tend to employ highly paid expatriates but also a share of their profits will be transferred abroad. For countries that lack qualified bankers, however, these costs may be a worthwhile investment while building a local banking infrastructure.

Other lessons of the Guinean experience are negative. The first is that the closing of weak public banks can be extremely costly if the government attempts to pay depositors. Not only will the past poor financial performance make the closing expensive, but corrupt officials can dramatically increase the cost by creating fictitious deposits. This type of behavior can also happen within private institutions. The Guinean experience illustrates the need for close supervision of failing institutions and the vital importance of documentation to verify claims.

The final lesson is that there is no substitute for sound financial policies and an effective legal structure. Efficient banking and financial deepening cannot take place without them. While private institutions will probably be able to provide better services than public ones (because of the different incentive structures for management), the government policies under which banks operate are perhaps an even more important guide to their actions than is ownership structure. Accordingly, if desired financial services are not profitable because of the legal and economic environment, neither private nor public institutions will be able to provide them. If appropriate financial development is to occur, appropriate financial and macroeconomic policies must be maintained, and an effective legal structure must be implemented.

Jamaica:
A Successful Share Offering

SUMMARY

The Jamaican government sold a majority share (51 percent) of the National Commercial Bank (NCB) in December 1986. The public offering of J$90.6 million (U.S.$16.5 million) was the largest public enterprise divestiture in Jamaica's history. By all objective measures, the sale was a clear success. The offering was oversubscribed by 170 percent; it attracted more than 30,000 stock purchase applications from Jamaican citizens and institutional investors; and it raised the bank's stock price by as much as 67 percent on the first day it was traded on the Jamaican Stock Exchange.

THE FINANCIAL POLICY CONTEXT

The financial system of Jamaica is moderately developed. Capital and money markets by no means offer the breadth, depth, and level of sophistication present in industrial country markets, but the basic institutional and functional structure is in place. It revolves around a diversified set of financial institutions, consisting of the Bank of Jamaica, commercial banks, merchant banks, development banks, building societies, and credit cooperatives. Most of these institutions operate according to competitive conditions and market forces. The economy is highly monetized. In recent years, interest rates have been determined largely by supply/demand conditions.

The Jamaican Stock Exchange was established in 1969, but languished throughout the 1970s as a result of generally declining economic conditions, corporate failures, and nationalizations. The stock market then rose significantly in value and volume during the 1980s, but declined in late 1987 and early 1988, following worldwide trends. As of mid-1988, the stock exchange listed common shares for 38 companies, preferred shares for 7 firms, and debentures for 6 companies. Government securities are not listed on the exchange.

As in most developing countries, Jamaica's capital markets evolved at a slower pace than did other segments of the financial system. Corporate financing for medium and large scale firms has typically been managed through direct borrowing from domestic or international banks, retained earnings, or intercompany loans from parent firms. Securities markets have not played a major role in corporate financing. Smaller enterprises typically rely on internally generated funds or family savings.

Throughout the 1970s and early 1980s, the financial sector of Jamaica acted largely as a captive to inappropriate macroeconomic and external policies. The domestic capital and money markets were forced into financing parastatal enterprises and increasing government budget deficits. They enjoyed limited attractive lending opportunities due to a downward economic spiral caused by declining demand for the nation's traditional exports and by import substitution-based industrial policies. As a result, while the institutional structure of the financial system was essentially sound, it played a subordinate role to fiscal policies and government ownership decisions. It was, therefore, unable to carry out its necessary functions in the area of capital formation.

The sale of NCB was designed and implemented not as a component of any financial sector policy or reform, but rather as part of a general government strategy to reduce the role of government in the economy through the privatization of state owned and operated enterprises (SOEs). This explicitly stated strategy of Prime Minister Edward Seaga's government aimed at reversing the 1970s' trend of a rapidly growing public sector. A 1982 government study catalogued the existence of over 200 public enterprises and about 230 statutory boards or other agencies. These SOEs carried out a wide range of economic activities typically left to the private sector, from agribusiness to manufacturing to the provision of financial services. A World Bank study calculated that these enterprises accounted for over 20 percent of Jamaica's gross domestic product (GDP) and much of the government's rising fiscal deficit (about 18 percent of GDP in the late 1970s) could be attributed to operating losses generated by these enterprises.

The Seaga campaign platform included a pledge to reduce the government's role in the economy, to be accomplished in part by the divestiture of SOEs. Shortly after Prime Minister Seaga was elected, he created an informal Divestment Committee to review all candidates for privatization. In 1983, this Committee was succeeded by a more formal Divestment Secretariat, which was funded by the Agency for International Development (AID) and benefited from increased authority and a full-time staff.

By the mid-1980s, the government had taken several steps to divest SOEs through means other than direct stock sales to the public. Progress was relatively slow and was marked by several failed initiatives, but it proceeded with growing momentum. Approximately 80,000 acres of government-owned land was sold to private holders. Operating control of several large hotels was transferred to private companies through management contracts. Most of the country's agricultural marketing boards (59 out of 69) were leased to the private sector, and several forms of public services in Kingston were contracted out to private firms.

Jamaica's privatization strategy reached a watershed in 1986. Reflecting on the strong results of privatization in the United Kingdom and Canada and increasingly frustrated with Jamaica's piecemeal approach based on a complex, long-term plan, the Prime Minister and his advisors became convinced that a more active strategy was required. This approach revolved around the identification of SOEs with a reasonable chance of attracting private investors, and the public sale of these enterprises through stock offerings. The NCB was selected as the first candidate to test the new policy strategy.

FINANCIAL POLICY REFORMS

In the early 1980s, the Jamaican government was faced with a convergence of adverse economic trends that were caused by both domestic policies and external forces. These trends included rapidly rising levels of government expenditures and employment, high rates of inflation and unemployment, capital flight, and burgeoning levels of government and external indebtedness. To reverse these conditions, the government initiated a sweeping series of "structural adjustment reforms," supported by the World Bank, the International Monetary Fund, and bilateral donors. Actions that affected Jamaica's financial system included the following:

Exchange Rate Reform

Until the early 1980s, the value of the Jamaican dollar was pegged at U.S.$1.78. After a period in which several different approaches were tried, the government initiated a biweekly auction for foreign exchange in December 1984. This system was replaced by "flexible managed" rates. Combining devaluations of the Jamaican dollar (against the U.S. dollar) with depreciation of the U.S. dollar relative to other major currencies, the Jamaican currency depreciated on a real, effective basis by 36 percent from 1980 to 1987, thereby enhancing the competitiveness of Jamaican exports.

Separation of Monetary and Fiscal Policy

In the 1970s and early 1980s, excessive monetary expansion financed the large and growing public sector deficits, primarily through the vehicle of a government overdraft facility with the Bank of Jamaica. The natural results were increased price inflation, capital flight, foreign indebtedness, and a "crowding out" of the private sector from local capital markets. The Seaga government actively sought to break the monetary/fiscal policy interdependence by various structural adjustment measures, including tax reform and reductions in budget expenditures.

Operational Requirements for Banks

Due in large part to structural fiscal deficits, the government had imposed liquidity ratio and cash reserve requirements on banks, which effectively subsidized public sector borrowing. Commercial banks, for example, could only meet required liquidity ratios by purchasing low yielding government treasury bills, thereby forcing them to charge higher rates for commercial loans to the private sector. These "government financing schemes" were gradually eased as the government's overall deficit has been reduced from a high of 16 percent of GDP at the end of the 1980s to about 5 percent of GDP in recent years.

Industry Deregulation

While by no means targeted toward the financial sector, the government's efforts to deregulate commercial transactions have exerted direct positive impacts on financial operations. For example, the number of commodities subject to price controls had been reduced from 60 to 13.

Tax Reform

In early 1986, the government implemented the first phase of a comprehensive tax reform program. It included reductions in the highest marginal tax rates on personal income, elimination of certain tax credits, and a streamlined tax administration. Biases in favor of debt financing (versus equity financing) were reduced through the imposition of taxes on interest earnings. Corporate tax reforms, including a reduction of the maximum tax rate from 45.0 percent to 33.3 percent, were enacted in 1987.

External Debt Reduction

Jamaica had, by the early 1980s, generated a significant level of accumulated external indebtedness because of structural trade deficits and unrestrained government spending. A series of reforms were undertaken to correct the serious balance of payments and debt problems. The exchange rate system was reformed, and several import substitution policy biases against exports were removed. In early 1982 the government lifted some 60 quantitative restrictions against imports, the first step in a five-year program to eliminate as many trade restrictions as possible. The number of items subject to quantitative restrictions has been reduced from over 360 to under 90 since that time. Export promotion efforts, particularly for nontraditional exports such as light manufactures, have yielded positive initial results. In addition, progress has been made in liberalizing exchange controls on capital account transactions. A debt rescheduling strategy has been followed, and a debt-equity swap program was initiated in late 1987. Notwithstanding these achievements, the problem of outstanding external indebtedness remains the most serious constraint to Jamaica's long-term growth.

IMPLEMENTATION OF PRIVATIZATION

The Banking Institution Involved

The National Commercial Bank has a long-standing history of operation in Jamaica. It was initially established in Kingston as the Colonial Bank of London in 1837. The bank was acquired by Barclay's Bank of London in 1925, and Barclays owned and operated the bank for over 50 years. In 1977 the bank was nationalized, along with many other enterprises, by the government of then-Prime Minister Michael Manley. Its name was also changed to National Commercial Bank. At the time of nationalization, NCB was the second largest commercial bank in Jamaica, with total assets amounting to some J$236 million.

Over the ten-year period of government control, NCB achieved a modest record of profitability and growth, largely because the bank was not subject to strong government interference. The bank's top management team, many of whom had worked for the bank under its private ownership, successfully retained operational independence. The NCB was run as if it were a private corporation, receiving neither special treatment nor onerous requirements by the government. As a result, the bank continued to pay corporate taxes and play a normal role as financial intermediary and provider of financial services. The bank's deposit and loan base continued to rise through the early 1980s. Pre-tax profits increased to a peak of J$38 million in 1985.

The market-oriented management and financial performance of the NCB clearly strengthened the prospects for successful privatization. The earnings record suggested the promise of positive returns for prospective investors, and the absence of debt or a poor loan portfolio removed the need to deal with the typical problem of accumulated deficits. In addition, the quality of the bank's balance sheet implied that other than the one-time receipt of proceeds from the sale, the divestiture would not have a major impact on the government's fiscal position.

Rationale for the Privatization

As noted earlier, the stock sale of NCB was carried out as part of a general divestiture strategy developed by the Jamaican government. The goals of this strategy were established under "A Suggested Programme for the Privatization of Government Enterprises" submitted to the Cabinet by the Prime Minister in the spring of 1986. These objectives included the following items:

1. Improve the efficiency of the economy by placing more productive capacity under private control.
2. Develop the local capital market and stimulate the involvement of a large number of citizens in the free market system.
3. Encourage more private investment and reduce the "crowding out" effects of state ownership.
4. Reduce the fiscal deficit.
5. Raise foreign exchange in those cases where foreign investors would be permitted to participate in the privatization.

The choice of NCB as the test case was made not only to meet the general government objectives described above but also to serve as a model and standard for future privatizations. The NCB was the first privatization to be implemented through a public share offering. It represented the largest privatization undertaken to date since it would involve transactions estimated at between J$90 million and J$100 million. Therefore, the selection of NCB as a candidate was intended to meet several targeted goals.

The sale of NCB shares would provide a concrete example of a privatization that would distribute the ownership of a major Jamaican enterprise widely throughout the public. The transaction would also expand the size of the Jamaican Stock Exchange by approximately 10 percent, hopefully attracting a new class of investors and stimulating a new form of domestic savings and investment instrument. A successful transaction would expand public awareness and support for privatization as a desirable national objective, thereby providing a useful "demonstration effect." In addition, placing NCB under private control would yield efficiency gains for the bank itself, as well as directly reduce the role of the government in commercial activities. Finally, the effective spread of ownership among thousands of small shareholders would blunt potential criticism from the political opposition that privatization implied the sale of government assets to the economic elite in Jamaica.

Privatization Method Employed

From the outset, the strategy for "privatizing" NCB was a public sale of 51 percent of the bank's shares. The method revolved around a standard public issue, involving market valuation, distribution of prospectuses, a marketing plan, and a time-bound period for the offering to take place. Aside from these typical components of any public offering, a number of special features were included (described below) to take into account the objectives of the government and the fact that such a sale was relatively novel to Jamaica.

Implementation

The precise execution of the NCB privatization was strongly influenced by the meeting between a close advisor of Prime Minister Seaga and a British privatization specialist. The advisor had attended an AID-sponsored conference on privatization in Washington, D.C. in early 1986. The specialist, a former member of Prime Minister Margaret Thatcher's privatization team and currently on the staff of the London-based merchant bank N.M. Rothchilds, was a speaker at the conference. These two individuals developed a close working rapport and became core leaders of the implementation team. All the leading members of the team came from the private sector and had previous experience in relevant transactions. The institutions involved included Rothchilds, the Kingston office of Price Waterhouse and Company, attorneys from two of Jamaica's most respected corporate law firms, NCB management, and a team from the Jamaica Information Service, which was charged with carrying out the marketing campaign. Several specific steps were taken to prepare and execute the transaction.

Stock Transfer and Capital Injection: In June 1986, the shares of NCB were transferred from the office of the government's trustee, the Account General, to the National Investment Bank of Jamaica (NIBJ), the organization chosen to carry out the transaction. At that time, NIBJ also contributed J$20 million of new capital to NCB to improve the bank's balance sheet, which reflected a low capital/assets ratio in comparison with commercial banks in the private sector.

Prospectus Preparation: From August through October, the privatization team focused their energies on preparing NCB for sale. This task included the preparation of a comprehensive prospectus, 170,000 copies of which were distributed throughout the country.

Future Ownership Structure: The proposed strategy was for the outright sale of 51 percent of NCB's outstanding common shares, leaving 49 percent of the bank's stock in government hands. However, to complete the "privatization," the 49 percent government holding was transformed into non-voting shares, as specified in the prospectus, with the government legally committed to the gradual sale of its shares as circumstances and conditions permitted. This condition effectively eliminated the government's financial and operational control over the bank and assured future stockholders that NCB would be managed by and for the private owners.

Share Sale Marketing: The team faced an enormous obstacle in the guise of an almost complete lack of public understanding of the rights and responsibilities of corporate shareholding. Since the government sought to distribute the shares of NCB widely, it required a massive public education campaign. The marketing strategy included the use of radio, television, press conferences, audiovisual productions, and targeted briefings to such groups as the Jamaican Agricultural Society, the Jamaican Employers Federation, the All-Island Jamaican Cane Farmers Association, and the Private Sector Organization of Jamaica. The entire prospectus was reprinted by *The Daily Gleaner*, the national newspaper, one week prior to the offering. In addition, a special four-page brochure, "Questions and Answers About the Share Offering," was prepared and distributed widely, including a reprint by *The Daily Gleaner* that reached some 200,000 individuals. The marketing campaign was assisted by a strong degree of public awareness of NCB due to its nationwide branch network and record of profitability and professional competence.

Share Pricing: The task of setting an appropriate share price required balancing the need to set prices low enough to ensure a strong response against the objectives of maximizing revenue from the sale and avoiding charges that the sale was a "giveaway" of public assets. The team employed a traditional approach for valuing the share price. They first evaluated the past and prospective financial performance of NCB, using the private Bank of Nova Scotia as a comparative benchmark. They then decided to set the share price at a discount from that of the Bank of Nova Scotia according to the standard practice used when issuing stock heretofore untraded in the market. This decision was bolstered by the desire to assure wide shareholding and was also supported by the fact that NCB had been performing less profitably than other major commercial banks.

The share price was eventually valued at J\$2.95, representing a price/earnings (P/E) ratio of 7.6. The comparable ratio for other leading commercial banks operating in the private sector was 9.3. The lower price set for NCB shares established their competitiveness and provided clear incentives for potential shareholders.

Share Allocation: Well in advance of the share offering, the government determined and announced that the sale would give priority to small shareholders. This goal sought to diffuse politically-based criticism that control would be shifted to the nation's wealthier class. In addition, widespread ownership would minimize the prospects for another round of nationalization in the future.

To achieve this objective, a limitation of 7.5 percent of the issued capital of the NCB Group per individual or firm was established, even at the risk of an undersubscribed offering and proscribed future growth. In addition, the sale included an allocation scheme that gave preference to individuals seeking small lots of shares. If shares had been distributed on a proportional basis, each applicant would have received 35.5 percent of shares requested since the offering was oversubscribed by 170 percent. According to the formula used and described in Table A.4, however, applicants for 1,000 shares received their full request, whereas those applying for the largest block of shares received less than 9.0 percent of their request.

Employee Stock Ownership: The overall stock sale strategy included an attractive feature for bank employees to acquire shares. This plan included a small number of free shares (20), a matching share program (25 free shares for 25 shares purchased at the offer price), and share discounts and priority access. In addition, employees were eligible to obtain their allocations by borrowing directly from the bank via a J\$10 million Special Loan Fund. This financial package used the shares themselves for collateral, and employees could repay the Fund over a two year period through payroll deductions. As a result of these facilities, 98 percent of the NCB's management and staff participated, and these

Table A.4
Share Allocation Formula

Number of Shares Requested	Number of Shares Received	Plus (%)	Of Additional Shares Requested Up To:
1,000	1,000	85.0%	500 shares
1,500	1,425	70.0%	500 shares
2,000	1,775	45.0%	1,000 shares
3,000	2,225	35.0%	1,000 shares
4,000	2,575	25.0%	1,000 shares
5,000	2,875	20.0%	2,500 shares
7,500	3,325	12.5%	2,500 shares
10,000	3,638	9.0%	40,000 shares
50,000	7,238	9.0%	50,000 shares
100,000	11,738	8.5%	Of Remainder Applied for

employees became the largest group of shareholders in the bank, controlling about 12.8 percent of the voting shares after the public offering.

Distribution: Successful execution of the offering required an effective and far-reaching distribution system. The network utilized consisted of the local branches of the Jamaican Post Office plus the branches of eligible banks serving as the points of distribution and collection. This network resulted in a total of some 400 retail outlets for the stock sale.

RESULTS OF THE PRIVATIZATION

The public offering of NCB shares took place over a ten working day period in November/December 1986. The offering was 170 percent oversubscribed and all expectations regarding investor interest were exceeded. Over 30,000 citizens and institutions in Jamaica applied for shares.

NCB shares were first traded on the Jamaican Stock Exchange on December 23. Some 170,000 shares were traded. The price of shares closed at J$4.94, a two-thirds increase from the offer price of J$2.95, leading to observations that the initial value was underpriced.

A higher price would have increased the government's revenue from the sale. However, the primary goal was not revenue generation, but rather gaining public support. Therefore a low offer price was a wise strategy. Notwithstanding the comments regarding the offer price, the sale was judged a major success. A large government-owned and operated bank was placed back into private hands. The transaction indicated a successful experiment, the first public offering of its kind in Jamaica, which could be used as a model for future privatizations. The stock market benefited from the entry of thousands of new shareholders and participants and enjoyed a major increase in capitalization of the market. Finally, public suspicions concerning political interference in the transaction and misgivings over its feasibility were overcome by the careful manner in which the offering was implemented.

LESSONS AND APPLICATIONS

The NCB privatization example furnishes a number of useful lessons regarding strategies and tactics for the divestiture of public enterprises.

1. The privatization of a major financial institution through a "standard" public offering of shares can succeed. However, careful planning and execution are of critical importance in the areas of balance sheet enhancement, prospectus preparation, information dissemination and marketing, and retail distribution.

2. A principal ingredient underlying the success of the NCB transaction was the fact that the bank was well managed and enjoyed a proven history of profitable performance. It was not plagued by a poor loan portfolio, and it was operated efficiently even during its period of government ownership. The profitable performance was due at least in part to a wise government decision not to set interest rate ceilings but rather to allow banks to set rates at the levels needed to attract deposits and cover costs.

3. Public offerings of SOE shares can mobilize new domestic savings from even relatively poor societies, introduce new investors and investment instruments to the capital markets, and increase overall market capitalization. However, this outcome requires concerted educational and marketing efforts.

4. Equity market privatizations are not completely dependent on a highly developed, sophisticated capital market. Capital markets and privatization

are closely interrelated since investor confidence, the tax structure, monetary policies, and economic performance play important roles. However, the NCB divestiture was accomplished in a relatively thin equity market, evidenced by the fact that the transaction increased the stock market's capitalization by 15 percent.

5. Appropriate share pricing is a critical factor. Most objective observers would conclude that NCB's offer price was undervalued by traditional market standards, but this price was deemed necessary because the sale was innovative in the Jamaican context and success was crucial from a political standpoint.

6. Privatizations can represent an integral component of comprehensive structural adjustment activities. The sale of NCB generated U.S.$16.5 million for the government, which could then be used to reduce budget deficits. In addition, NCB has since grown and increased its profitability, thereby offering increased tax revenues to the government.

7. The chances of successful public offering divestitures are enhanced if the privatizations are preceded or accompanied by certain policy reform initiatives. Most analysts would agree that the sale of NCB probably could not have taken place in the early 1980s, when Jamaica was mired in declining economic conditions and a host of policy constraints. Improvements in the tax system, deregulation, trade and exchange policy reforms, and other measures taken in Jamaica prior to the offering created an atmosphere conducive for the successful private sector purchase of NCB. While no single policy change can be isolated as exerting a critical influence, the combination of reforms played a highly positive role in setting the stage for the privatization.

Mexico:
Breaking Down the Barriers to Entry

SUMMARY

The Mexican government has traditionally played a large role in the national economy, owning and operating a number of monopolies such as petroleum refining and distribution, certain mining activities, railroads, forestry, and radio and television, and competing with private enterprises in areas such as retail food stores and cinemas. In 1982, in the midst of a foreign exchange crisis, the government added banks to its list of state-owned enterprises.

Because the underlying economic and foreign exchange difficulties remain unresolved, and because the government and the nation are accustomed to extensive government ownership of the economy, the banking sector remained basically in government hands prior to 1991. As Figure A.1 shows, more than 92 percent of all financial assets were owned by government-controlled financial institutions prior to 1991. The government monopoly on commercial banking functioned as "the ultimate barrier to entry." No private commercial banks were allowed to operate. Even before the nationalization, Mexico had stiff barriers to foreign banks. Citicorp was the only foreign bank allowed to operate.

Three types of partial bank privatization have occurred in Mexico. The first type, the emergence of privately-owned brokerage houses to rival the nationalized banks in providing money and portfolio management services to large depositors, has been credited with increasing the competitiveness of banking and inducing the government-owned banks to introduce several attractive new instruments. The second type of partial privatization ocurred in 1987, when the government sold 34 percent of the capital in the banks to the private sector. Because the sale left operational control and decision-making in the hands of the government, few direct results were expected. The banks did have a larger pool of loanable funds as a result of the capital infusion. In addition, employees, many of whom chose to purchase stock, had greater incentives now that they benefit directly from profits. The third type of privatization was initiated in 1990, with the government's announcement that it planned to privatize its 18 state-owned banks.

Figure A.1
Government Control Over Principal Financial Sector Assets

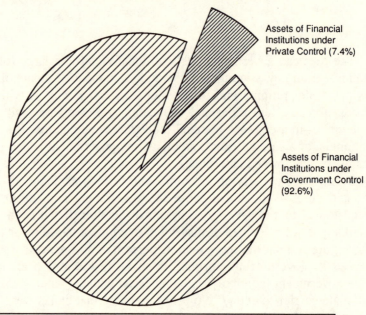

Assets of Financial
Institutions under
Private Control (7.4%)

Assets of Financial
Institutions under
Government Control
(92.6%)

Institution	Assets ($ Billions)	Percent of Total Assets
GOVERNMENT CONTROLLED	**52.3**	**92.6**
Multibanks	35.6	63.0
Nacional Financiera (Nafinsa)	16.0	28.3
Insurance Companies*	0.7	1.2
PRIVATE SECTOR CONTROLLED	**4.2**	**7.4**
Mutual Funds*	2.3	4.1
Brokerage Houses	1.9	3.3
TOTAL	**56.5**	**100.0**

* Shared government and private sector control.
 Source: SRI Estimates. All figures as of December 1986.

FINANCIAL POLICY CONTEXT

On September 1, 1982, in the face of a foreign exchange crisis, President Lopez Portillo of Mexico issued a decree nationalizing the banking system. The Mexican peso had depreciated by nearly 400 percent during the year, rising from 26 pesos to the U.S. dollar in January 1982 to nearly 100 pesos by December. Foreign exchange reserves plummeted from more than $4 billion in 1981 to less than $900 million in 1982. The trade and the current account balances had deteriorated steadily over the previous five years; 1981 ended with deficits of $4 billion and $14 billion, respectively. Inflation was edging toward an annual rate of 100 percent, and real gross domestic product (GDP) was stagnated.

In this deeply troubled economic context, the Federal Government nationalized the banks in order to preclude widespread bank failure and stem the flood of foreign exchange overseas. The only banks not nationalized were Mexican branches of representative offices of foreign banks and Citibank N.A. (the only full-service foreign bank allowed by the government to operate in Mexico). The decree was formalized on December 30, 1982, in the "Public Service Banking and Credit State" (Ley Reglamentaria del Servicio Publico de Banca y Credito).

The decree compensated the private owners of nationalized banks with long-term bonds that were issued in August 1983 and mature in 1992. The Bank Indemnification Bonds (Bonos de Indemnizacion Bancaria, or BIBs) were secured by the Federal Government and tradable on the stock exchange.

Prior to the nationalization, Mexico had an impressive array of specialized financial institutions. The financial system consisted of 60 commercial banks, several dozen savings and loans, and approximately 20 development banks and trust funds that funneled subsidized credit to high-priority sectors. Savers could choose between a variety of fixed and floating rate instruments, including government bonds and commercial paper with maturities ranging from three months to 12 years.

When the banks were nationalized, the government announced it would "preserve the administrative autonomy of each bank in order to foster competition, creativity and efficiency in their operations." Beginning in 1983, however, the government began consolidating the institutions. Within three years, the government had reduced the number of banks from 60 to 19. By 1990, the financial structure consisted of six nationwide banks and thirteen regional and multi-regional banks. They had a total of 4,500 branches and approximately 185,000 employees.

The banks were complemented by general and specialized development banks and trust funds, all owned and operated by the government.

FINANCIAL POLICY REFORMS

Since the nationalization, the Mexican Government moved to improve bank supervision. In December 1984, the Mexican Congress passed a new package of financial legislation that increased the powers of the Central Bank to regulate the banks. The law and its regulations established strict operating rules, including capital/asset ratios, portfolio diversification standards, and limits on investments in individual firms. The law also established ceilings for domestic credit and government debt.

The government had not shown any interest in reducing its control over credit allocation. The 1984 law reduced the reserve requirement (the percentage of selected liabilities that banks must hold with the Central Bank), an important improvement, but it also increased the percentage of total credit that must be channeled toward "priority sectors." The new legislation decreased the reserve requirement from 50 percent to 10 percent of eligible liabilities, allowing banks to increase their lending. Unfortunately, the law also provided for more government control over bank lending portfolios by raising the percentage of total lending that must go to sectors chosen by the government.

IMPLEMENTATION OF PRIVATIZATION: 1987

Through 1990 all banks were still majority government owned. However, partial privatization has occurred in Mexico in the last several years. In 1987, the government laid the initial framework for this privatization by authorizing the sale of 34 percent of the capital in each nationalized bank to private hands.

Private individuals and businesses could choose between two instruments offering them ownership in the banks: equity shares (certificados de aportacion patrimonial) and subordinated convertible debentures with a five-year maturity. The shares, which provide their owners full voting rights and limit their liability to the value of the share, were traded on the Mexican Stock Exchange. The debentures are convertible to voting shares on the occasion of each interest payment (4 times a year). The debentures are subordinated; in case of liquidation, debenture owners receive payment only after all other debt obligations have been paid but before shareholders. The debentures pay an interest rate based on the market rate for Mexican Treasury bills.

Only Mexican nationals, 100 percent Mexican owned firms, and Mexican local governments or parastatals could purchase the new instruments. Individuals and private firms were limited to a 1 percent share of each institution and government and parastatals to 5 percent.

Two of the largest banks, Bancomer and Banamex, were the pioneers in selling the new instruments. Bancomer raised $36.7 million by selling 2.4 million shares and 1 million debentures, each priced at 24,000 pesos ($10.52 U.S. dollars). Banamex increased its capital by $42.0 million, offering 5.2 million shares and 3.5 million debentures, each at 11,000 pesos ($4.82 U.S. dollars).

The prices were set by each institution at such favorable terms that the offerings were almost completely subscribed on February 4–6, 1987 by clients, management, and staff at the banks. The remaining instruments were sold on February 6 through the Mexican Stock Exchange, creating a functioning secondary market in the securities.

The second form of privatization now under way is the emergence of privately owned brokerage houses as providers of certain financial services. Since the nationalization in 1982, brokerage houses (*casas de bolsa*) have grown dramatically both in size and in breadth of activities to rival the nationalized bank for large deposits. The rise of the private brokerage houses has already brought about a noticeable increase in the efficiency and dynamism of the Mexican financial markets.

The privately owned brokerage houses buy and sell stocks and money market instruments, manage mutual funds (on their own and their customers' behalf), and organize transactions in commercial paper. In a real sense, the brokerage houses are operating increasingly as banks *for large savers.*

The brokerage houses have been growing rapidly. The 26 casas de bolsa managed $8.3 billion in funds in 1986, up from $6.4 billion the previous year. The number of accounts rose from 118,066 to 186,023 over this same period. To administer the growth in activity, brokerage houses increased the number of their employees from 4,822 in 1985 to 7,008 in 1986, and expanded their branch network. They have also been highly profitable. Profits rose from $33 million in 1985 to $44 million in 1986, representing a 30 percent return on capital.

One reason for the expansion of the brokerage houses was the high level of activity on the stock market, until the stock market dropped in 1988. However, a more fundamental structural driving force has been the nationalization of the commercial banks. Prior to the nationalization, wealthy individuals and executives of private firms often established proprietary relationships with their bankers. Following the government takeover, these individuals could no longer be assured that their banking relationships and transactions would remain proprietary. Therefore, they have increasingly turned toward the services of privately run brokerage houses. At the same time, while the management quality of commercial banks has deteriorated, the brokerage houses have attracted the more qualified and entrepreneurial professionals who seek higher salary structures and more operational flexibility.

The government response to the rapid growth of the private brokerage houses had been one of careful observation but no intervention. Insofar as they are competitors of the government-owned banks in offering money and portfolio management services to large depositors, the government is watching the brokerage houses carefully. Knowledgeable observers suggest that the government views privatization of the government banks as politically unfeasible, but it is pleased with the emergence of the private sector alternative to the banks.

RESULTS OF NATIONALIZATION AND PARTIAL PRIVATIZATION

Results of Nationalization

Nationalization has had several negative implications for the Mexican financial sector. In response to the nationalization of banks and strict credit controls, firms were increasingly turning to other companies for financing. The growing intercompany loan market operated through brokers, who place promissory notes with cash-rich companies. Free from government interest rate controls, both borrowers and lenders obtained more favorable terms dealing directly with one another rather than through the banks, thereby leading to financial "disintermediation." The nationalized banks were losing customers and fees as firms sought alternative methods of financing growth.

A second negative effect of nationalization has been reduced bank profitability. In 1985, Mexico's nationalized banks posted a return on assets of only one-half of one percent. Mexico's largest three banks, Bancomer, Banamex, and Banca Serfin, held more than half of commercial bank assets, and have posted reasonable profits in recent years. The smaller regional banks were either breaking even or losing money. The poor financial performance of the banks was to a certain extent a reflection of the weak condition of the Mexican economy as a whole.

However, this situation has been aggravated by a general deterioration in the banks' quality of service since they were nationalized. With the possible exception of the three largest banks, observers indicate that most banks have experienced a decline in the quality of their professional staffs. Salaries declined in real terms, and staff members were no longer eligible for subsidized loans, which had been a powerful financial incentive. Banking procedures reportedly became more bureaucratic in nature.

On a positive note, it seems that favoritism and "less-than-arms-length" transactions have abated since the nationalization. It is not clear why government officials would have fewer incentives than their private sector counterparts to engage in these kinds of activities, especially if their compensation packages are lower. However, the general consensus in Mexico is that there is less corruption in the banks now that the government is the owner.

Results of Partial Privatization

The emergence of the private brokerage houses generated benefits for the Mexican banking system, as the nationalized banks were forced to compete for large deposits and the accompanying fees by offering attractive new instruments.

In what could be taken as an effort to lure back some of the large savers to the nationalized system, the government ruled in early 1986 that banks could issue Bankers Acceptances (BAs) and could set the rate of interest on them. These instruments were similar to the Certificates of Deposit issued by U.S. banks. Mexican banks and savers responded enthusiastically to the expanded use of Bankers Acceptances, and the value of BAs in circulation doubled in real terms in 1986, to $1.7 billion. For purposes of comparison, time deposits in Mexican banks (which do offer real positive interest rates) totalled $11.6 billion in February 1987. Savings accounts, which paid a low, fixed rate of only 20–25 per year (while inflation is estimated at 100 percent per year), had attracted only $775 million as of June 1986. Another innovation by two of the largest banks was the introduction of "Master Accounts," or checking accounts that paid money market rates. Thus, the private "banks" were a force for innovation and high quality service within Mexico's nationalized banks.

Some observers were concerned about what they considered lax supervision of the rapidly growing brokerage houses as well as the intercompany loan market. The brokerage houses fell under the purview of the National Securities Commission, which also regulated the stock exchanges and the mutual funds. The Commission's staff of 300 was generally regarded as highly qualified, nonetheless there was some concern that the brokerage institutions do not receive the appropriate level of oversight relative to their growing importance in the financial markets. Intercompany loans are completely unregulated.

In 1990, Mexico repealed its 1982 bank nationalization law and initiated efforts to privatize its 18 state-owned banks, the third form of privatization. The privatization plan is part of a larger initiative to move the Mexican insurance, stockbrokering, banking, and other financial service industries into larger, more unified financial groups that will help to form a Mexican universal banking system. These new banking groups will also be expected to forge links with international banks through minority equity participation if privatized.

Mexico's plan calls for controlling 51 percent shares to be sold to groups of Mexican citizens, while foreign investors may purchase up to 30 percent. It is hoped that the government's 66 percent ownership in these commercial banks will net it between $3.5 billion and $6.5 billion. After the privatization program was announced, interest rates decreased and investor interest in the stock market increased.

By June 1991, the first two sales had already taken place. Multibanco Mercantil de Mexico and Banpais sold for approximately $385 million, about three times their book value. The new owners claim that they intend to convert the banks into multipurpose, European-style financial firms offering bank, brokerage, and insurance services. In August 1991, a controlling interest (31 percent) was sold in Banamex, the country's largest bank, to a group of private investors for $3.18 billion.

LESSONS AND APPLICATIONS

Mexico's 1987 privatizations offered several important lessons for other nations. Mexico successfully sold 34 percent of its two largest banks to management, employees, clients, and other individuals and firms. The shares were priced attractively to assure a successful sale. The partial privatization increased the amount of loanable funds available to the banks as well as increased the management's and employees' incentives to run an efficient operation. The partial privatization is serving as a first step toward the eventual return of the banks to private hands.

Mexico has also seen the rise of a dual banking system. Privately owned brokerage houses have increased in size and breadth, and intercompany loans have increased. The emergence of the private alternatives for large depositors and large borrowers has put pressure on the nationalized banks to offer quality service and attractive instruments.

The entrance of alternative instruments and institutions has a negative side. Some observers are concerned about a lack of supervision of the brokerage houses and intercompany loan markets. As savers and borrowers increasingly turn to the private alternatives, it is imperative to assure that the newly emerging institutions and markets are adequately supervised. If the "neophyte" institutions and markets are appropriately regulated and reviewed, they offer a powerful force for competition and efficiency within a newly revitalized banking system.

The Philippines:
Dismantling Government Domination

SUMMARY

In 1980-1981 the Philippines instituted several banking reforms, such as the liberalization of interest rates and establishment of universal banks (unibanking), that caused increased savings mobilization, growth in commercial bank deposits and credit, and a lengthening of loan maturities. Unfortunately, these reforms were insufficient to prevent the financial crisis of 1983-1984, which resulted in the acquisition of failing commercial banks by the government. Since President Aquino took office in 1986, several of these commercial banks have been fully divested and one additional bank has been partially divested through the government's privatization program. The Philippine National Bank, which accounts for one-quarter of all commercial banking activity, remains to be privatized. Unibank formation continues as a trend, with 12 such banks now in operation.

THE FINANCIAL POLICY CONTEXT

The banking system of the Philippines is historically one of the most competitive and highly specialized in Asia. The banking sector is composed of nearly 1,500 institutions, including private and government-owned commercial banks, savings and mortgage banks, savings and loan associations, private and official development banks, and rural banks. The non-banking sector comprises investment houses, finance companies, insurance companies, and a number of other non-bank financial institutions.

The Central Bank has the overall responsibility for regulation and supervision of banking as well as non-banking institutions. The Department of Commercial and Savings Banks conducts regular examinations of over 1,200 institutions. The Department of Financial Intermediaries regulates the operations of all institutions performing quasi-banking functions.

The basic monetary policy followed by the Philippine authorities has been to increase private sector credit levels while restraining inflationary pressures. The Central Bank controls the money supply and credit conditions by dealing in government securities, setting commercial banks' reserve requirements, imposing selective credit controls, and adjusting its rediscount rates. It also influences credit markets through compulsory cash deposits on imports.

Two government-owned financial institutions have played major roles in implementing government policy. The Philippine National Bank (PNB) and the Development Bank of the Philippines (DBP) were used by the government policy makers because they could provide services that private sector banks, due to market imperfections, were not willing to provide. Together these two banks have accounted for up to one third of all resources in the financial system.

The PNB, established in 1916, grew to become the largest commercial bank in the country, holding approximately one fourth of all deposits in the commercial banking system. The PNB had the same powers and functions as any other commercial bank, but because of its size and government ownership it also served as a tool for implementing government economic policy.

Since 1975, commercial banks have been required to maintain a minimum paid-in capital of 100 million pesos. This requirement resulted in a number of domestic mergers and affiliations with U.S., Japanese, and European banks. Foreign banks are allowed to hold equity positions of up to 40 percent of the voting stock of a domestic commercial bank.

Prior to 1981, the Central Bank set maximum interest rates on various types of loans. The overall savings rate was low and loan maturities were generally short term. The lack of long-term credit stemmed primarily from the legislated specialization of the financial institutions. Even institutions designed to specialize in long-term credit, such as investment houses, dealt primarily in high interest, short-term credit and money market operations.

FINANCIAL POLICY REFORMS

Beginning in 1981, the Philippine financial system underwent a series of policy changes aimed at making the system more streamlined and efficient. The Monetary Board approved a number of circulars intended to allow market forces to determine interest rates. Virtually all forms of deposits and loans with maturities in excess of one year became free of interest rate ceilings. Loans with maturities of less than one year remained subject to interest rate ceilings set by the Central Bank.

To increase the supply of long-term credit, the government also began a series of reforms to increase competition among banks and foster greater efficiency in the financial system. The most significant reform was the introduction of the "unibanking" concept, which allowed eligible institutions to engage in a range of financial activities.

These financial reforms, primarily the liberalization of interest rates and lifting of restrictions on commercial banking activity, were quite successful. The volume of savings increased rapidly in the 1980-1983 period; commercial banks' deposits and credit outstanding increased, and a significant lengthening of loan maturities was achieved.

These reforms, however, were mostly curtailed because of overriding economic events. A massive investment program to utilize non-petroleum energy sources and excessive lending to businesses owned by cronies of President Marcos led to the near-collapse of the financial system. A significant event contributing to the weakening of the financial system was the assassination of opposition leader Benigno Aquino. This event ignited enormous capital flight, signaling a lack of confidence in the political and economic system.

The major deficiency in the financial system that contributed to the 1983-1984 banking crisis was the poor performance of the PNB and the DBP. Their portfolios became clogged with non-performing assets (NPAs). Observers raised serious questions regarding their extensive role in the economy. In practice, the PNB and DBP competed with private banking institutions and actually impeded the private banks' development.

During the subsequent financial crisis, the government took control of many troubled firms. As a result of acquisitions made during the financial crisis of 1983-1984, the government came to own seven commercial banks that competed with 28 private, domestic commercial banks. During the process of financial consolidation, monetary policy was disregarded on numerous occasions through the government's emergency liquidity assistance to ailing businesses and government investment programs. Monetary policy came completely unravelled in 1984 when the money supply was allowed to grow by 50 percent, causing interest rates to peak at 45 percent in June of that year.

In October 1983, the government placed a moratorium on principal payments of foreign debt, and in the next month launched extensive foreign exchange controls, including the requirement that banks turn over their foreign exchange to the Central Bank. These moves were in response to the massive capital flight following Aquino's assassination. The economy underwent a period of considerable financial shallowing: savings fell to an all-time low, credit to the private sector severely contracted, and real interest rates rose sharply.

One of the most disturbing features of the Philippine financial sector was the high spread between commercial deposit and lending rates, averaging about 16 percent, whereas in most countries spreads range between 3 and 4 percent. The main cause of high intermediation costs is the implicit and explicit taxation on banks. These taxes include high reserve requirements, forced investment in agrarian reform bonds, and inflation. There is also an explicit tax of 5 percent on gross receipts plus a tax on profits. The high spreads could be reduced by lowering the reserve requirements, increasing interest paid on reserves, and eliminating the agricultural bonds requirement and the gross receipts tax.

It is important to note that the trend toward unibanking, a financial policy initiated during the Marcos period, has continued. Nine unibanks were in operation as of February 1984; that number had increased to twelve as of February 1988. With traditional banking becoming less profitable through stiffer competition and with a political situation that favors long-term commitments, more and more banks have turned to investment banking to diversify their services and remain competitive within the industry.

IMPLEMENTATION OF PRIVATIZATION

Several banks continued to experience liquidity/solvency problems after being acquired by the government. These banks had been originally taken over because they were in serious danger of failure. The government intended to sell them back to the private sector after rehabilitation. However, the rehabilitation was unsuccessful and their condition deteriorated further.

When President Aquino took over in early 1986, the government was burdened with an estimated 330 government-acquired corporations of all types, the vast majority of which were insolvent. Included among these corporations were six commercial banks. Many of the corporations designated for privatization were included in the portfolios of the Development Bank of the Philippines (DBP) and the Philippine National Bank (PNB) as non-performing assets.

In August 1986, President Aquino approved the Government Reorganization Plan and named an interministerial Committee on Privatization (COP) whose main task was to formulate policies and guidelines governing privatization. An Asset Privatization Trust (APT) was established in December 1986 to be the disposal entity for major state-owned enterprises. The first step in the privatization process was to formulate a privatization plan for a specific state-owned enterprise, either by the responsible government department or by the APT. The plan was then forwarded to the COP for approval. Initially, the preparation/study phase for divestiture candidates was carried out carefully, and potential buyers were provided with comprehensive background materials. Eventually, motivated by the desire to speed up the privatization process, the government changed its selling approach to an "as is, where is" basis.

The government of the Philippines signed an agreement with the World Bank in which the latter agreed to provide $310 million in development credits. The agreement was conditioned, however, on the privatization of all six government-acquired commercial banks by October 1988, a condition that as of July 1991 has not been fully met.

The Financial Institutions Involved

Among the six government-acquired commercial banks, three have already been partially or completely divested to the private sector, and the government has plans to privatize two additional institutions. The status of each privatization is described below:

1. *International Corporate Bank* (Interbank)—Size: P579M paid-in capital
   Status: Forty percent was sold to American Express International Banking Corp. on July 4, 1986, through a debt to equity conversion. Some 59.7 percent is still held by the National Development Company (NDC), a government entity. The remainder of less than 1 percent is held by Philippino investors. As of September 1988, the COP has designated NDC to act as the disposition entity for Interbank and to draw up a detailed privatization plan. American Express expressed interest in purchasing a 30 percent share of the Rizal Commercial Banking Corporation (RCBC) for the purpose of merging it with Interbank. This move would allow RCBC to go into unibanking, while holding total American Express equity below the government limit of 40 percent ownership by foreign banks.

2. *Commercial Bank of Manila*—Size: P322M
   Status: The government shareholdings were fully disposed of and the new private shareholders took over management of the bank on December 11, 1987. Among its shareholders are the First National Bank of Boston, Three Eight Corporation, Ace Solid Holdings Corp., and Cabien Corporation. The First National Bank of Boston purchased $19 million by converting into equity some of its Philippine debt that had been blocked since the imposition of a debt moratorium by the Central Bank in 1983. The purchase will allow the U.S. bank to upgrade its operation in the Philippines to a fully licensed local bank able to lend in pesos. Bank of Boston will supply

management expertise. The U.S. bank cannot repatriate its investment until 1991.

3. *Pilipinas Bank*—Size: N/A

   Status: In March 1988, the government signed an agreement disposing of its shareholdings in Pilipinas Bank to Prudential Bank and Bank of Tokyo. The former owner of the Pilipinas Bank was suing to delay the sale of that institution. As of October 1988, it appears that the suit will be dismissed, allowing the APT to proceed with the sale before year-end.

4. *Union Bank of the Philippines*—Size: P500M

   Status: Land Bank (a government bank) holdings in the Union Bank (39 percent) were sold to the Aboitiz Group of Companies on August 31, 1988. Union Bank increased its authorized capital from 500 million pesos to 1 billion pesos, although it was undergoing privatization. At least 20 percent of the bank's new shares were set aside for sale to its employees and to the general public. Union Bank is profitable, posting a P32 million in the first quarter of 1988.

5. *Associated Bank*—Size: N/A

   Status: APT is currently preparing a privatization plan and will act as the disposition agency for Associated Bank.

The Philippine National Bank and the Republic Planters Bank have been directed to draw up their own divestment program in preparation for eventual privatization. The PNB privatization is now scheduled for discussion with the COP. Both banks have a positive net worth, although Republic owes the government P238 million.

Rationale for Privatization

The Philippines Government is carrying out a major government enterprise sector reform. The government intends to withdraw from the provision of all marketable goods and services. In a May 1986 speech to the 19th Annual Meeting of the Board of Governors of the Asian Development Bank (ADB), President Aquino stated that "this regime means business when it says it will not meddle in private business. Government will provide the usual public services and facilities, preserve order, vindicate rights and protect liberties. But the private sector should be the main propeller of the economy. I believe that the restoration of a genuine private enterprise economy will foster competition, productivity and efficiency." As commercial banking is often considered an area of private sector activity, the privatization of these banks plays an important part in the overall government restructuring strategy.

Privatization Methodology Used

The government shareholdings in the above-described banks were fully or partially disposed of through private sale agreements. The agreements were based on offers made in an auctioning process administered by the APT. No attempts have been made to issue shares for sale to the public.

Implementation of Privatization

In the cases of the Commercial Bank of Manila, Pilipinas Bank (once the lawsuit is settled or dismissed), and Union Bank of the Philippines, the privatization process was or will be completed through a full disposition of the government holdings. For the International Corporate Bank, about 40 percent of the government holdings was sold. The COP has designated the National Development Company (NDC), which still holds 59.7 percent of the stock, to act as the disposition entity for the bank. The privatization plan for the Associated Bank is being drawn up, and the privatization of Philippine National Bank is scheduled for discussion with the COP. The privatization of the Republic Planters Bank has yet to be undertaken.

RESULTS

Banking reforms instituted prior to the financial crisis of 1983-1984 yielded good results in terms of increased savings, commercial bank deposits and credit, and longer loan maturities. The privatization of individual government-held banks is viewed as a positive sign. The greatest impact, however, will come from the disposal of non-performing assets of the Philippine National Bank and the eventual divestment of the bank itself.

It appears that in the privatization of the banks, the government is selecting groups with considerable experience in banking to take-over the operations. Perhaps this approach can avoid problems caused by inexperienced management in running financial institutions. The utilization of debt-equity swaps in the privatization of the government-acquired commercial banks, if implemented appropriately, can serve as a means to reduce external debt.

References

Arthur Young. "Interest Rate Controls and Financial Repression in Developing Countries." Preliminary draft prepared for the U.S. Agency for International Development, February 4, 1987.

Aylen, Jonathan. "Privatization in Developing Countries." *Lloyds Bank Review* (January 1987): 15-31.

Barchard, David. "Trusting the Market." *Financial Times*, September 16, 1987.

Barletta, Nicolas A., Mario I. Blejer, and Luis Landau, ed. "Economic Liberalization and Stabilization Policies in Argentina, Chile, and Uruguay: Applications of the Monetary Approach to the Balance of Payments." The World Bank, Washington, D.C. (1983).

Beesley, Michael, and Stephen Littlechild. "Privatization: Principles, Problems and Priorities." *Lloyds Bank Review* no. 149 (July 1983): 1-19.

Brown, Kevin. "Unique Business Experiment: National Freight Corporation." *Financial Times*, September 16, 1987.

Brucato, Peter F., Jr., and David G. Davies. "Property Rights, Managerial Behavior, and Firm Performance: A Study of Government and Privately-owned Banks in Australia." Unpublished paper, 1990.

Bureau for Program and Policy Coordination, U.S. Agency for International Development. "Financial Markets Development." AID Policy Paper, Washington, D.C., August 1988.

Bureau for Program and Policy Coordination, U.S. Agency for International Development. "Implementing A.I.D. Privatization Objectives." AID Policy Determination, no. 14, Washington, D.C., June 1986.

_____. "Private Enterprise Development." AID Policy Paper, revised; Washington, D.C., March 1985.

Cowan, L. Gray. "Privatization: A Technical Assessment." Report prepared for the U.S. Agency for International Development, Washington, D.C., September 1987.

Dale, Richard. *Bank Supervision Around the World.* New York: The Group of Thirty, 1982.

Davis, David G. "Property Rights and Economic Behavior in Private and Government Enterprises: The Case of Australia's Banking System." *Research in Law and Economics*: 3: 1981: 111–142.

Dooley, Michael P., and Donald J. Mathieson. "Financial Liberalization and Stability in Developing Countries." Unpublished manuscript for IMF Working Paper, International Monetary Fund, Research Department, March 17, 1987.

E. F. Hutton & Company, Inc. "Alternative Financial Instruments for Less Developed Countries." Report prepared for the U.S. Agency for International Development (June 1987).

Edward, Howard. "Conference Paper: A Successful Approach to Privatization." Excerpts from a trip report, June 29, 1987.

Edwards, Howard, and Enrique Garciq-Ayaviri. "Divestiture of Targeted State-Owned Enterprises: Grenada." Prepared by the Center for Privatization for the Bureau of Private Enterprise, U.S. Agency for International Development (April 1987).

Fry, Maxwell. *Money, Interest, and Banking in Economic Development.* Baltimore, Maryland: The John Hopkins University Press, 1988.

Goldsmith, Raymond W. "The Quantitative International Comparison of Financial Structure and Development." *Journal of Economic History* 35, no. 1 (March 1975): 216–37.

Gordon, David L. "Development Finance Companies, State and Privately Owned: A Review." World Bank Staff Working Paper no. 578, Management and Development Series no. 5; The World Bank, Washington, D.C. (1983).

Graham, George. "How the Paradox Unwound: Profile: Mr. Edouard Balladur." *Financial Times*, September 16, 1987.

Granzow, Herman. *"La Politica de Privatizacion del Gobierno Chileno."* Santiago de Chile, Octubre 21, 1987.

Green, Keith B. *Financing Development in Latin America.* London: MacMillan, 1971.

Hanke, Steve H., ed. *Prospects for Privatization,* Proceedings 35, no. 3; New York: The Academy of Political Science, 1987.

Hanke, Steve H., ed. *Privatization & Development.* San Francisco: Institute for Contemporary Studies, 1987.

Hanson, James A., and R. Neal Craig. "Interest Rate Policies in Selected Developing Countries, 1970-82." *Industry and Finance Series* 14; The World Bank, Washington, D.C. (1986).

Hemming, Richard, and Ali M. Mansoor. "Is Privatization the Answer?" *Finance & Development* 25, no. 3 (September 1988).

The Heritage Foundation International Briefing. "Privatization: Lessons From British Success Stories." no. 15; The Heritage Foundation, Washington, D.C. (February 1987).

Hinds, Manuel. "Financial Crises in Developing Countries," Country Economics Department, Financial Systems and Policy Division, The World Bank, November 18, 1987.

International Financial Statistics, Supplement on Public Sector Institutions, International Monetary Fund, vol. 13 International Monetary Fund, Washington, D.C. (1987).

Jonquieres, Guy de. "Competition Still the Issue: U.K. Experience." *Financial Times*, September 16, 1987.

Lewis, Vivian. "France's Nationalized Banks—A Whiff of Re-Privatization," *The Banker* 130 (July 1980): 43–48.

Litan, Robert E. "Evaluation and Controlling the Risks of Financial Product Deregulation." Reprint from the *Yale Journal on Regulation* 3, no. 1, (1985).

The MAC Group. "Capital Markets and Privatization." Report prepared for the U.S. Agency for International Development (May 1987).

McLindon, Michael P. "Macroeconomic Aspects of Privatization: The Case of Jamaica." Paper presented at the Privatization Strategies and Techniques for Development Seminar, Washington, D.C., July 1, 1988.

_____. "Privatization in Jamaica." U.S. Agency for International Development, Jamaica, October 1987.

Mansoor, Ali M., and Richard Hemming. "Privatization and Public Enterprises." International Monetary Fund Occasional Paper no. 56 (January 1988).

Mohsin, Khan S., and Nadeem Ul Haque. "Capital Flight From Developing Countries." *Finance & Development* (March 1987): 2–5.

Nankani, Helen. "Techniques of Privatization of State-Owned Enterprises." World Bank Technical Paper no. 89, vol. 2; The World Bank, Washington, D.C. (1988).

O'Brien, Richard, John Calverly, Sarah Hewin, Ingrid Iversen, eds. *Privatization: A Powerful Worldwide Trend*. The Amex Bank Review 13, no. 10; London: American Express Bank Ltd., 1986.

Pauley, Robin. "A Universal Desire to Reduce Role of State." *Financial Times*, September 16, 1987.

Roth, Gabriel. *The Private Provision of Public Services in Developing Countries*. Published by the Oxford University Press for the World Bank, 1987.

Shirley, Mary M., and Elliot Berg. "Divestiture in Developing Countries." World Bank Discussion Papers no. 11; The World Bank, Washington, D.C. (1987).

Sundararajan, V., and Lazaros Molho. "Financial Reform and Monetary Control in Indonesia." Unpublished manuscript for IMF Working

Paper, International Monetary Fund, Central Banking Department, January 20, 1988.

Talt, Nikki. "City Coffers Enriched: Professional Services." *Financial Times*, September 16, 1987.

Thomas, David. "Public Backlash Against BT: U.K. Telecommunications Companies." *Financial Times*, September 16, 1987.

Velasco, Andres. "Liberalization, Crisis, Intervention: The Chilean Financial System, 1975-1985." Unpublished manuscript for IMF Working Paper, International Monetary Fund, Central Banking Department, July 21, 1988.

Vickers, John, and George Yarrow. *Privatization: An Economic Analysis*. Cambridge, Massachusetts: MIT Press, 1988.

Virmani, Arvind. "Government Policy and the Development of Financial Markets: The Case of Korea." World Bank Staff Working Papers, no. 747; The World Bank, Washington, D.C. (1985).

Vuylsteke, Charles. "Techniques of Privatization of State-Owned Enterprises. " World Bank Technical Paper no. 88, vol. 1; The World Bank, Washington, D.C. (1988).

Wellons, Philip, Dimitri Germidis, and Bianca Glavanis. *Banks and Specialised Financial Intermediaries in Development*. Paris: Development Centre of the Organisation for Economic Co-operation and Development, 1986.

White, David. "The Socialist Sell-Off: David White Explains the Paradoxes of Spain's State Disposals." *Financial Times*, September 16, 1987.

The World Bank, "Financial Intermediation Policy Paper." Industry Department, Washington, D.C. (July 8, 1985).

Young, Peter. "Privatization in LDCs: A Solution That Works." *Journal of Economic Growth* 1, no. 3; National Chamber Foundation, Third Quarter 1986.

Index

About the Authors

NEAL S. ZANK is associate director of the National Commission for Employment Policy. He is the author of a number of articles and book chapters on financial markets and privatization. Mr. Zank served previously at the U.S. Agency for International Development.

JOHN A. MATHIESON is director of the International Policy Center of SRI International. He is the co-author of two books, *The United States and the Third World* (1982) and *Struggle Against Dependence: Nontraditional Export Growth in Central America and the Caribbean* (with Kathleen D. Vickland, 1988).

FRANK T. NIEDER is Senior International Economist with the International Policy Center of SRI International—Washington. He has worked extensively on macroeconomic, finance, and trade and investment promotion issues in developing countries.

KATHLEEN D. VICKLAND is Senior International Economist with the International Policy Center of SRI International—Washington. In addition to co-authoring *Struggle Against Dependence*, she has authored several articles and papers on economic development issues.

RONALD J. IVEY is a Senior Manager with Ernst and Young's International Management Consulting Group. He has extensive experience in privatization and private sector development in developing countries.